Joined-up Governance

Making sense of the role of the school governor

Jane Martin and Ann Holt

Second edition

Adamson Publishing

Copyright © Jane Martin and Ann Holt, 2002, 2007

Reprinted 2008 with amendments

Published by Adamson Publishing
8 The Moorings, Norwich NR3 3AX
tel: 01603 623336 fax: 01603 624747
e-mail: info@adamsonbooks.com

ISBN 978 0948543 17 3

British Library Cataloguing in Publication Data
A catalogue record for this book is available from the British Library

Cover design by Judith Robertson

Printed and bound in Great Britain by Marston Book Services Limited, Oxford

Contents

Introduction

All governors will be familiar with the much-repeated statement that they form the largest volunteer workforce in the country. There is no question on the census form about whether you are a governor, so the exact numbers are not known, but it is certainly around one third of a million people in England and Wales.

If that sounds like an army, then the size of the task explains why it is needed. Those governors are spread over some 24,600 schools, which accommodate over 8 million pupils. That is over 8 million children aged between five and sixteen, whose future lives governors are intimately involved in shaping. The money that is spent on education in England alone is £60 billion (figures for 2006–7), the total amount in the UK being 5.6 per cent of the gross national product. Although not all that money goes direct to schools, in England the sum that does works out as an average of £2910 per primary school child per year, and £3800 per secondary school child (government figures for the year 2004–5). That volunteer army is responsible for how this money is spent.

With these sorts of figures it is not surprising that so many members of the public are involved in school governance. But people do not volunteer because of the size of the task, they volunteer because the 8 million plus are all individual children – their own children, their neighbours' children or the children of their community. The money is for their future.

For local people acting as lay governors, the school system, and the educational world more generally, can appear complex at best, confusing at worst. Many a governor has bemoaned their lack of educational expertise. Overlay that with complicated questions of governance and for many it becomes difficult to put their original motivations to support pupils into the reality of practice. We know that governors ask themselves: "What exactly is my role? What am I here to do?" And even when those questions are answered: "How can I make an impact?" This book helps to answer that question by giving governors a focus for their work.

We know governors come from all walks of life. You operate in a wide range of different environments: community schools, foundation schools, voluntary aided schools, voluntary controlled schools, primary, secondary and special schools, specialist schools, academies, trust schools, training schools, schools with Charter Marks, schools in Education Action Zones and schools in Excellence in Cities programmes. Some of you are in leafy suburbs, some in seriously deprived neighbourhoods. Some of you can easily attract the best teachers and considerable funding, some of you find it difficult to fill vacancies and set a budget at all.

You will all have had to get to grips with the National Curriculum and the plethora of tests and exams: SATs at 7, 11 and 14 (in England), GCSEs, AS level and A levels, and vocational qualifications. You will try to keep on top of the increasing statutory responsibilities. There has been a string of Education Acts with increasing frequency from 1986 up to today, most of which have had several clauses affecting how schools are to be governed. Each of them has made the educational world a more bewildering and alarming place for the layperson.

However, few involved in schools would want to go back to pre-1986 days, when governors' powers were very limited, governing bodies were composed on party lines and parents had no voice in how their children's schools were run. Nor would anyone claim that there is any quick fix that can make all schools and the whole system perfect. Few would argue against the values of diversity, allowing all schools to develop their own character. While most governors would welcome the political spotlight being turned somewhere else, so that the pace of change could become less feverish, few would deny that a level of change is a fact of life. Our world is changing very fast, and education needs to be responsive.

All this provides the context in which governors do their work. There can be no doubt that many governors feel daunted by the array of things for which they are responsible. Some also feel undervalued by the politicians who seem to forget that governors are completely unpaid and motivated by a sense of public service. To many governors it can feel that they have been placed in the middle of an educational labyrinth and are looking for the golden thread to find their way around.

Being a governor need not mean being anything like as overburdened and perplexed as some people suggest. Certainly, being a governor is not easy, and no one should pretend that it can be. But it can be a lot simpler than it is often made out to be. There is a purpose behind the responsibilities, and there is a rationale for the duties. The secret of effective governance is to be guided by some key principles that help you see the wood from the trees.

As authors of this book, between us we have many years' experience of being governors and supporting governors. We know that time is precious and effective governance means focusing on the things that really matter and make most impact. Being a school governor is certainly a duty, but it is also a privilege. We want to help governors enjoy what they do, to feel fulfilled from a job well done, and to make best use of their limited time.

In the chapters that follow we have outlined what to us are the key principles that underpin governance and make sense of the job. We believe that understanding those principles will help make it easier. From that understanding come practical ways of keeping focused on the job of shaping a successful future for your school and its pupils.

We have called this book "Joined up Governance" because we believe that making links between the key principles and essential tasks can help you and your colleagues do more of what makes for a successful future and less of what can be better done by others or not done at all. A system of local democratic governance of education should empower local people to make an active contribution, and we hope this book goes some way to support that endeavour.

The governor's role 1

If you are a governor yourself, or a teacher or a headteacher, there will almost certainly have been a time when you will have asked yourself the question, "Why do we have governors?" After all, in the history of our state education system the current system of governing schools is a recent phenomenon. It was introduced in only 1980, and even then the full panoply of statutory powers was not granted to school governors until 1986. Yet governors are now a significant feature of the educational landscape, and there is undoubtedly a recognition that public participation in the way schools are governed is here to stay.

Despite the considerable powers given to governors, what we should do and how we should do it has very much been open to question – not least as the government has introduced more and more legal duties without taking much away. The cry has gone up more than once that volunteer governors cannot hope to fulfil the duties required – that the job is now too large and requires specialist knowledge and a lot of time. Certainly, there is an urgent need for school governors to work differently – to focus clearly on the key responsibilities that are essential to being an effective governor. But this does not mean doing more; in fact, it should mean doing less, but doing it with a purpose and confidence that not only support and develop the school but connect it more readily with the community it serves. This chapter sets out the fundamental principle of why we have school governors and defines the role and how it should be carried out.

Why have school governors?

Public accountability

"Public schools" in the United Kingdom are elite fee-paying establishments to which in the main only the better-off can afford to send their children. The majority of our children are educated within "the state system", the education system run by the state. What is taught in our schools is set within a framework prescribed by the government, teachers are employed and paid by the state, and our schools are built and funded by the state, sometimes supported by benefactors, as with Academies. But the state runs the system on behalf of the public. In this sense state schools are "public" schools.

Funded by taxpayers' money, schools offer an education to the children of the citizens of the state – hence, they are providing an essential public service. Free education for children from five to sixteen is an essential, if not *the* essential, public service in a free and democratic society. The idea of this public good not being available to us at the beginning of the 21st century is ridiculous. Moreover, what is taught in our schools, how and what our children learn, and how the education they receive is organised and delivered, are of public concern – not only to the parents, but to all of us, and in particular to local communities and employers. From a wide range of perspectives, we all want a society where our children are educated to be happy and fulfilled individuals, to be worthwhile members of society, of the community, of the family and of the workforce. Indeed, as taxpayers we want to be sure that our money is being put to good use.

The public needs to know, and has a right to know, what is happening in our schools. There is a legitimate public interest in state education. Therefore the state education system has to be accountable to the public – the public has a right to affect how things are going. In other words, there has to be public accountability. This is the reason why we have school governors.

Representing parents, teaching and non-teaching staff, the local authority (LA), the local diocese or church, the local community, and other benefactors, school governors are the voice of the public in our schools. A public service must be run in the interests of the public it serves, and those who manage the public services need to be informed by those who best know the needs of the public. Moreover, the public that pays for the service must have confidence in it, and when it comes to schools, parents who use them should be able to trust them to do the best possible job.

Just as good private organisations use market research techniques to stay "close to the customer", it is no longer good practice for public services just to be run by "detached" professionals reckoning to know best the public's wants and needs. Yet education is more than a product on the supermarket shelf, so market research techniques are themselves inadequate. More sophisticated methods are needed to produce a dialogue between school managers and the public. The governing body is the appropriate mechanism for this. Indeed, because the concept of a market in education is irrelevant for many families and communities, we can see even more the importance of a dialogue between the governing body and the school, as this is an effective means of developing trust in the institution.

> *School governors are the bridge between the school and the community. They are the legitimate voice of the public in decision-making that affects how schools are run and what they should be in the future.*

So what do we *not* have school governors for? We do not have them to manage our schools – headteachers and their senior staff do that. We do not have them to inspect our schools – the Office for Standards in Education, Children's Services and Skills (Ofsted*) does that. We do not have them to run our schools – teaching and non-teaching staff in schools do that.

Asterisked terms are defined in the Glossary, on pages 116–21

Could public accountability be exercised some other way? Don't local elected councillors have the right to question what goes on in our schools on behalf of their constituents? Don't we elect Members of Parliament to represent the views of the public to the government about what they are doing? And shouldn't parents go directly to the school if they are unhappy about something to do with their own child? Certainly these are ways in which members of the public, directly or indirectly through representatives, can and do seek information and present concerns at a local or national level. But these are inadequate on their own. The first two are too remote, likely to be retrospective and influenced by other concerns. The last one is too individual, and only answers specific grievances.

Local management of schools

Nowadays schools are more and more in charge of their own destiny. The introduction of a partially elected governing body in every school in 1980 was a response to concerns that schools were unaccountable to the public. Until then schools were run by the professionals – the local education authority had formal responsibility from the Secretary of State for Education for the administration of schools locally and appointed their headteachers. But there was no local accountability as neither Whitehall nor the town hall were close enough to exercise it. As the public mood shifted away from the post-war disposition to vest authority in the professional classes in the faith that they would bring about "the good society", so there was also a change in education policy.

This shift saw the 1980 change in arrangements for school governance being followed up with a new system for managing schools. Under the now familiar local management of schools*, decisions about how each school should be run and developed are taken locally by the governing body, instead of, as previously, by the local education authority for all its schools. This is a system of local school-based decision-making by those local stakeholders* who should know best how to use resources in the most efficient way. The new system had another aspect, which earned it characterisation as "the hub and the rim" of a wheel, as local management of schools (the rim) was followed by greater prescription over what was to be taught (the hub). Local decisions about use of resources were soon being made within the centralised framework of the new National Curriculum*, which determined what was taught in the classroom.

This stakeholder system has developed over the 1990s and the 2000s as local management has developed, with schools having much more responsibility for their budget, their staff, their buildings and for delivering the curriculum*. Although local management also saw powers passing from local authorities to headteachers, education legislation has accorded much of the new responsibility to governing bodies. The power to make the broad, strategic decisions about what goes on in our schools lies not with the headteacher or teachers alone, but with the public's representatives – the governors.

These changes do not, however, mean that local authorities have been removed from the picture. Responsibility for schools is still legally held by LAs, but is formally delegated to the school governing body. For this reason the local authority has reserve power to remove delegation from a school governing body and take responsibility for the school itself, if the governing body fails to exercise its authority in line with statutory requirements. So, although individual governors are elected by different constituencies or appointed by different bodies, as a corporate body their legitimacy comes from the local authority. As we will see, the legal responsibility of the LA is far from nominal and is an important one.

It is important not only for governors but for headteachers and teachers to understand why there is a need for school governors. The governing body has a number of statutory duties or functions, and these are underpinned by this prime purpose of exercising public accountability. Accountability is also the reason why a system of local democratic decision-

Why governors?

→ page 12

Statutory responsibilities

The governing body has a number of statutory responsibilities:

- *conducting the school with a view to promoting high standards of educational achievement*
- *setting targets for pupil attainment*
- *deciding in broad strategic terms how the school should be run*
- *managing the school's budget*
- *making sure that the curriculum is balanced and broadly based, that the National Curriculum and religious education are taught, and reporting on National Curriculum assessment and examination results*
- *determining the staff complement and a staff pay policy for the school, and implementing and maintaining the Workforce Agreement*
- *appointing a new headteacher or deputy, when necessary*

Based on A Guide to the Law for School Governors

making in our schools has been introduced that allows local people to participate and contribute to decisions about their local school – a public service run by the public, for the public, in partnership with the professionals who serve the public.

What is the governors' role?

Despite the volume of legislation and regulations affecting school governance it is a common complaint, not least among governors, that the role of the governor is unclear. At the outset of local management in the 1980s, there was a strong movement towards governors acting as quasi-managers. Governors with particular skills were openly sought to help with financial management and marketing, and many a bank manager found that he or she was being asked to join their local governing body to chair the finance committee.

Governors consequently tended to become involved with non-educational matters, such as premises issues, as many of them felt more comfortable with these than with those closer to the heart of education. Opening up the "secret garden" of the curriculum to lay governors was not an easy job and many teaching professionals found themselves spending fruitless time on such a task. Information and training sessions on the National Curriculum provided by governor training and support from local education authorities helped break down the barriers.

Although governors have accepted a wider role since the early days of local management, and most have been able to get a grip on the many statutory responsibilities handed to them, and have exercised them carefully and rigorously, it has still been difficult to see how those responsibilities add up to a clear role. More importantly, it has been difficult to know quite how to go about exercising responsibility. The biggest question of all has been trying to gauge reasonable levels of the knowledge, expertise, skill, time and energy required to do a proper job.

Raising standards

The School Standards and Framework Act 1998 and subsequent regulations* went a long way towards clarifying what governors should be doing. This Act put the governor's role in the context of the government's drive to improve schools and pupil performance.

"Raising standards" might seem to be a finite task, related only to academic performance and presupposing a level at which exam results have got as good as can realistically be expected. But this is not the real point of this much repeated exhortation. For one thing, the quality of education offered by a school cannot just be measured in academic results. But more importantly, behind this upwards drive is the recognition that in a rapidly

> "The governing body shall conduct the school with a view to promoting high standards of educational achievement at the school."
>
> School Standards and Framework Act 1998, *para. 38*

changing world education cannot stand still. Schools need to adapt to change, and, even better, to anticipate it. No school can therefore remain where it is; it will either improve or deteriorate. The primacy then of seeking improving standards comes about through a recognition that schools need to look at how they do things, because what worked well ten years ago, or even last year, cannot be relied on still to work well tomorrow.

How should the role be carried out?

There are four key principles upon which the role of the school governor is based:

- The governing body only has statutory authority as a *corporate body*.

- The essential role of the governing body is *strategic* not operational.

- The most effective approach of the governing body is to be a "*critical friend*" to the school.

- The recommended working practice of the corporate governing body is to *delegate authority* to individuals or groups of its members to carry out functions on its behalf.

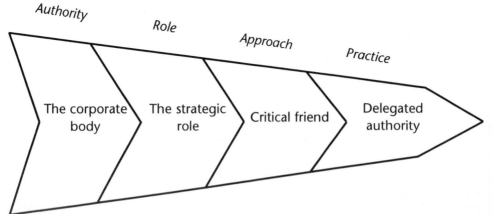

The four principles of the role of the governor

The four roles were clarified in Terms of Reference Regulations* promulgated in September 2000 (since amended) and feature in *A Guide to the Law for School Governors* * and other government publications. The following text investigates and explains each one in turn.

School governors have no authority as individuals. The statutory authority is vested in the corporate governing body. This means that any decisions are taken or policies agreed by the whole governing body, or by a committee empowered to act on the governing body's behalf. This also means that as long as the governing body is always careful to act in good faith on the best information available to it, any liability also stays with the corporate body. As individuals we are not personally liable for any actions properly carried out on behalf of the whole governing body.

The corporate body

Individual governors or groups of governors, therefore, have no rights to take decisions, nor can they assume responsibilities, unless specifically authorised to do so by the full governing body. The only exception to this is the chair of governors, who can take decisions in certain circumstances requiring urgent attention. These are true emergencies only (a situation that poses an immediate threat to the well-being of a pupil, staff member, parent or the school) and will be rare. Any action taken by the chair on behalf of the governing body, whether delegated or an emergency, must be reported back to the next full governing body meeting and formally recorded. If a chair is routinely reporting chair's action* this is a sign that the governing body is not working properly, nor according to the regulations.

The corporate body must work as a team in sharing the workload. This means making sure that all governors are encouraged to make a contribution. It also means that business should be organised so that all governors are kept fully informed, and can participate in policy formulation and review and in key decision-making.

Chair's action

"The chair or vice-chair has the power to carry out functions of the governing body if a delay in exercising a function is likely to be seriously detrimental to the interests of the school, a pupil at the school or their parents, or a person who works at the school."

Guide to the Law, *chapter 3, para. 3*

When you remember why the governing body is made up the way it is, this stricture about individual action makes sense. The *raison d'être* of the governing body, and the entire basis of its authority, is that it is not a collection of individuals, however gifted, but is representative of the school's stakeholder groups. It is a corporate body where representatives of the stakeholder groups discuss and agree the future direction of the school. What is important is securing that agreement. Even if some governors have to agree to disagree, they should abide by the corporate decision.

The principle of working as a team in a corporate body is exemplified by the need for proper quorate meetings at which a majority of governors are present to take key decisions. The current regulations state that one half (rounded up if relevant) of the current number of governors must be present and voting for a decision to be valid.

The strategic role

The Terms of Reference Regulations 2000* set out the respective roles and responsibilities of governing bodies and headteachers (with some amendments made in 2003). They clearly state that the role of the governing body is strategic. Government guidance (DfEE 2000) defines such a role as "setting up a strategic framework for the school, setting its aims and objectives, setting policies and targets for achieving the objectives, reviewing progress and reviewing the strategic framework in the light of progress". What does this mean in practice?

In an important study of how governing bodies should work, *Lessons in Teamwork* (1995), the Audit Commission talked about the "steering" role as one of the key roles of the governing body. The role focused on agreeing aims, values and policies for the school. The word "steering" has since normally been replaced by "strategic", but the difference is slight. Steering and strategy are both to do with setting a course, deciding on a route, looking to the future for the school, thinking about what the school needs to achieve and plotting how to get from where it is now to where you would like it to be in the future. This does not mean that the headteacher and staff do not also think strategically. Indeed, strategy must be worked out in partnership – and the vast majority of headteachers who choose to be governors, together with governors representing the teaching staff, have a legitimate role to play as part of the corporate body in setting the course.

The Terms of Reference Regulations make it clear that creating strategy is the essence of the governing body's role. It produces the strategy for the school's development. Management of the school is not your responsibility, but belongs to the school's senior staff. But what does being strategic mean in practice?

Playing a strategic role means first and foremost setting out aims and values for the school.

Aims and values

Although some aims and values seem to be self-evident, identifying them can often be a hard job. Most of us could happily sign up to the aim: "creating a successful school where all pupils reach their full potential". But what that means for different pupils in different schools can vary. In a school where most pupils regularly achieve a high degree of exam success, reaching full potential may well focus on "rounding out" the educational experience in terms of music, drama or sporting achievement. In schools where academic success is less easily achieved across the board, a wide variety of academic and vocational curriculum goals may be more appropriate. A "coasting school" with consistently good examination results might need to ensure that all pupils are being supported with their learning needs, including both the gifted and those with special needs. For

→ page 55

specialist schools and schools with a religious denomination, the way in which the governing body works to support all pupils will reflect their particular curriculum specialism or faith.

Governing bodes can often be made up of people with different perspectives, so discussions of the aims do not always easily lead to consensus. However, it is the *process* of reaching agreement that is the key, and it will keep you on track as you plot the strategic route. The discussions may well be more important than the outcome, because it is in having these discussions that you confront the unstated ideas that you have about the school.

When finalised, a school's aims and values are often encapsulated in a mission statement.*

The strategic framework

Fulfilling the strategic role is a three-stage process. The first is deciding on the aims and values, the second working out how to put these into practice, and the third ensuring that they *are* put into practice. A key document in the second and third stages is the School Development Plan.*

The School Development Plan (SDP) – or School Improvement Plan (SIP)* – provides the strategic framework for the school. The plan should be owned by the governing body: the headteache usually draws it up, but it is up to the governing body to approve it and to be sure that it represents what the governing body wants for the school. The plan sets out the key priorities for the school, how resources are going to be used to support those priorities, and the tasks or action plans needed to achieve the improvements required, together with dates and the people responsible for carrying them out. It is linked with other key policies.

The school improvement planning process, and the policy-making process associated with it, will form the annual cycle within which the governing body reviews and evaluates success in achieving its priorities. Chapter 2 sets out the way in which "joined-up" governance can fulfil this role within a

---

Examples of mission statements

Placewell School aims to serve its community and, in partnership with the community, aims to produce confident, responsible, well-educated students who can fulfil positive roles in society.

We strive to achieve this by providing a caring environment where excellence and equality can develop through high-quality learning experiences based on individual needs and abilities.

*

We are committed to involving all pupils, parents, staff and governors in providing a broad and balanced education which encourages the pursuit of excellence, both moral and intellectual, and which values effort as well as recognising achievement.

---

clearly defined statutory framework. This planning process is the critical tool in "doing" strategy – but what precisely is our role?

Thinking and acting strategically

As we saw earlier, it is not the role of the governing body to manage the school – directly. It is not, moreover, the role of the governing body actually to construct the SDP. It is certainly not the role of the governing body to put together the tasks or actions that are required to achieve the plan's priorities. The role of the governing body is to bring a strategic view and to provide a forum for strategic thinking about the future of the school – in this planning process and in everything else they do. In practical terms the governing body brings the strategic perspective to the development plan, by checking and challenging how it fits with the mission, ethos and aims of the school.

It is a good device to regard the development plan as the strategic route map to achieving the improvement priorities for the school. It is the role of the governing body to check out that the route is the best way to get there. In essence this means asking three key questions:

Example of acting and thinking strategically 1

Governors on an interview panel bring the wider strategic perspective to the selection process by considering how the candidates could bring appropriate and complementary skills and experience to the school as a whole, and thus support its aims and values.

• Does the map acknowledge the same priority "destinations" as the school's mission and aims?

• How does this map get us where we want to go?

• Is this the best route in terms of making use of resources and building on existing strengths? And if not, how can extra resources be marshalled?

From these big strategic questions detailed discussions on options and timescales will naturally follow – but much of this should rightly be left to the senior management team. You should have the confidence to engage in rigorous strategic discussions on the plan – which may result in rethinking and amendments – before the operational detail is worked out by managers and staff for final discussion and ratification.

When this role is carried out effectively the governing body is not only responding to one of its key functions, it is also providing an important support to headteachers and senior staff. Any governors who fear that they might be treading on their toes should bear in mind that discussing the SDP is often the only opportunity the school's senior staff have to reflect on their decisions and plans within the wider context of the community and the local authority. It thus might be the only occasion they can view their school from the different and wider perspective of the public they serve.

There are two key characteristics of strategic thinking. Thinking strategically means:

• being clear that the key focus of priorities and decisions is in line with the aims and values of the school

• considering strengths and weaknesses and suggesting what the school should keep doing, what should be improved, what should be changed, and what the school should stop doing.

The governing body is not just a debating chamber. As well as thinking about strategy, it needs to act in a strategic way, so as to see that its decisions are followed through. In other words, it does not just think strategically, it acts strategically. What this means can be summarised in three points.

Acting strategically means:

- ensuring the school is managed in keeping with the strategic framework by requesting reports and reviews

- being involved in key interventions along the route, such as the performance review of the headteacher

- bearing the wider picture in mind in discussions and decision-making and not getting lost in the detail of tasks and actions; this is operational and should be left to the headteacher and staff.

> ### Example of acting and thinking strategically 2
>
> *In setting the objectives for the head, the governors conducting the head's performance management review consider the aims expressed in the SDP to ensure that the head concentrates on working towards achieving them.*

A critical friend

Nobody can have been a governor for long without having heard the term "critical friend". It has been current for some years, and was given legitimacy in the Terms of Reference Regulations of 2000 confirming that the recommended approach of the governing body was to act as a "critical friend" to the the headteacher. This is the way in which we can fulfil our purpose of exercising public accountability.

The governing body, and every governor, must start from a position of being a friend to the school – someone who supports, offers constructive advice, can be used as a sounding board for ideas, gives a second opinion and just offers help where it is needed. A friend who is critical also has the skills to challenge sensitively, ask questions or seek information to ensure the best ideas and solutions are arrived at in line with the strategic framework. As with the strategic role, critical friendship should not be seen as a restriction on the powers of the school's management, but as a beneficial quality which the governing body brings to decision-making and policy development since it allows the headteacher and appropriate staff to reflect on their own practice in a sympathetic and stimulating environment.

The governing body can only become an effective critical friend when there is an open and trusting relationship between the governors and the headteacher, based on mutual respect for what each brings to that relationship, and a willingness to be constructive at all times. Where there is no respect and trust, the critical friendship can turn into excessive scrutiny, which can be construed as a threat.

Seeking information We should always try to be reasonable in seeking information and should give fair notice of our requirements. In a constructive relationship the headteacher would not be asked to provide any information which he or she would not be using for their day-to-day management functions. Effective governance requires information, but in a manageable flow, not in torrents. Moreover, we should expect to be in contact with a range of senior staff in exercising this function, not just the headteacher.

Challenge or scrutiny? Challenging ideas and proposals does not mean that a headteacher should have to defend or justify every proposal he or she brings to the governing body. And remember that being concerned with strategic thinking does not mean having the

---

"Heads should give their governing bodies enough information for the governors to feel confident that those delegated responsibilities – and the head's own responsibilities – have been met. Governing bodies should make sure they get enough information to allow them to check on their school's achievements and progress, over time and in comparison with similar schools."
Roles of Governing Bodies and Head Teachers (*DfEE Guidance 0168/2000*)

headteacher explain every operational detail. A challenge from a governor should usually relate to the wider strategic framework or key development priorities. Questions that seek clarification can be helpful but not if details of management functions are repeated and combed through.

A confident headteacher will always invite questions and find challenge stimulating. They will always be willing to answer questions and provide information where the request is reasonable. But challenge should always be on a professional basis and should focus on the area under review – personal challenges, for example regarding the headteacher's competence, would be quite out of order in a public forum. A confident governing body will give the headteacher the space to manage but will expect to hold them to account on how they manage within the strategic framework, not on operational details. Its members will learn to exercise the appropriate degree of challenge and not descend into excessive scrutiny, which can be counter-productive and destructive of trust.

Delegated authority

The governing body has a number of statutory responsibilities to carry out which require time and energy. Some of these must be exercised by the full governing body, but the remainder are usually delegated to a committee, a working group, an individual governor or the headteacher. Indeed, it is recommended working practice that the governing body should delegate much of its work to others. The Decision Planner on the DCSF governors' website indicates what can and cannot be delegated; details of what has to be handled by the whole governing body are given on the next page.

It is important to understand, however, that functions and responsibilities that are delegated are done so on the authority of the corporate body. It is therefore critical for the full governing body to ensure that it has working procedures that not only cover all the statutory responsibilities but which also are clear and transparent to all. It should

Items that have to be dealt with by the whole governing body

appointing a headteacher or deputy (though the selection process must be delegated to an appointments panel)

appointing the chair or vice-chair

appointing community and other coopted governors

delegating functions to committees or individuals

drawing up or amending the instrument of government

fixing dates of governing body meetings

regulating governing body procedures

removing community governors

removing the chair or vice-chair

drawing up or reviewing annually the terms of reference of committees and selection panels

suspending governors

the constitution of the governing body itself

Items that can be delegated to committees but not to individuals

approving the annual budget

changing the category of the school

determining the admissions policy (foundation and voluntary aided schools)

framing a discipline policy

ratifying or countermanding the exclusion of a pupil

hearing an appeal by a teacher against dismissal or a pay or promotion decision have clearly defined mechanisms to ensure that the full governing body is kept informed of how groups or individuals are exercising the authority that has been delegated to them.

There are three main rules:

- The governing body cannot delegate authority for responsibilities which the law states remain with the full governing body or which have to handled by a committee such as an appeals panel.

- The governing body may delegate all other responsibilities to the headteacher, an individual or a committee. Within the regulations that determine what may be delegated to heads and what to committees, it is up to the governing body to decide on whether to delegate and, if so, to whom. The governing body should set out the terms of reference or remit within which such delegated authority should be exercised – which must be complied with. This is particularly important for financial delegation. It means that the headteacher must comply with any reasonable direction from the governing body in connection with delegated authority. The terms of reference should include reporting procedures so the governing body can ensure that delegated authority is being exercised properly and reasonably.

- Governing bodies have no authority to direct the headteacher over any function or responsibility which legally rests with him or her.

Delegation is essential to ensure the smooth running of the governing body. Indeed, for most governing bodies, delegation to committees* and working parties* has become the only way to get through the business. It is not, however, mandatory to have committees, and some governing bodies, usually those of small schools, do not have them but conduct their business in full governing body.

As well as being practical, delegation to committees is also

Committees and working groups

an important way in which the governing body team can ensure that all members share the load, and in so doing, become active and develop particular skills and expertise. A good chair of governors will see it as an important part of his or her job to ensure that functions and responsibilities are delegated in such a way as to involve all members of the governing body.

Wherever delegated authority resides, much of the business of the governing body should be done in partnership with the headteacher or with their senior staff in an advisory capacity. Indeed, for many statutory responsibilities the governing body or the committee will rely heavily on the headteacher or staff to prepare much of the work and give advice on which decisions can be based. The DCSF's → page 23 Decision Planner referred to earlier sets out the respective responsibilities of the governing body and the headteacher.

Committee membership and terms of reference* must be reviewed annually – you may include people who are not members of the governing body as associate governors and can decide whether or not to give them voting rights on the committees. You may also decide that they can attend governing body meetings, but they cannot have a vote there.

When delegating to sub-groups the distinction between a *committee* of the governing body and a *working party* is important. A committee is recognised as a legal entity because it has executive authority or responsibility which it exercises on behalf of the corporate governing body. As such the composition and constitution of a committee must be approved by the full governing body, and the committee exists for as long as it has that approval. Usually committees continue to operate over a long period.

Working parties, however, focus on a particular task or are discussion groups, or both. They have no formal responsibility, although they will be given a remit by the full governing body to carry out tasks on their behalf. Crucially, a working party cannot make a decision on behalf of the

---

Questions to ask when deciding on delegation to committees and working groups

What specific legal responsibility/function(s) is being delegated?

What decisions will the committee/individual/working group be empowered to make?

What is the proper composition of the committee in terms of representation, skills, expertise or experience?

Is it an advantage to have associate members on the committee – and if so with what representation, skills or experience?

How will the committee do its business, and who will clerk it?

What is the timetable for decision-making?

What is the mechanism for ensuring all governors are aware of how delegated authority is being exercised?

Is this the most efficient and effective way of handling this responsibility?

---

governing body whereas a committee can. A working party can only make a recommendation. The arrangements as to who attends a working party and how it conducts its business are less formal and need not be subject to the same scrutiny and regulation; non-members of the governing body can participate as fully in their work as governors, as working groups do not have decision-making powers.

There are several questions that you need to ask when considering what functions to delegate. These are listed above.

Finally, there are some restrictions on who may serve on certain committees. The most important of these is that staff governors (teaching or non-teaching) may not sit on any committee that has the powers to confer a benefit on them. This clearly refers to a staff salary committee. It also means

Restrictions on committee membership

that a staff governor should not be on an appointments panel in certain situations – notably, if one of the candidates is senior to them in the same department, and the governor would stand to be offered that candidate's job should the candidate be appointed to the post in question. Also staff members cannot be among the governors appointed to conduct the headteacher's performance management* review. With these exceptions, staff governors have the same rights to sit on committees as other governors.

The rule of not being in a position to benefit from the work of the committee applies to all governors. For example, a governor who ran a building firm that was applying for a contract to do building work in the school could not take part in any committee while it was involved in making the decision.

The whole point of delegated responsibility is to ensure that responsibilities are exercised by the most appropriate people in the most efficient and effective way. It is therefore important to ensure that committees and individuals with delegated authority do not make more work for themselves, the headteacher or the governing body. It is important that they are allowed to get on with taking decisions they have been authorised to take. As statutory authority rests with the corporate body, committees or the headteacher should always report their decisions back to the governing body, but not so that they can be discussed again – they are a matter of report only. Only if a committee or the headteacher appears to be acting outside of the authority delegated to them by the governing body should decisions be challenged. It is, however, perfectly legitimate to ask why a particular decision was made.

For more information on committees and recommended structures see chapter 4.

Individual governors need to recognise the importance of their contribution to the work of the corporate governing body. Each will bring to it a distinctive public voice. In the following chapters we go on to explain how effective governance can be focused in practice. However, it is important to remember that as governors you are there primarily to ensure the many voices of the public are heard, and that your authority is delegated from the local authority – and ultimately from the Secretary of State for Education — to inform the strategic direction of the school in the best interests of the local community.

In order to ensure that all the voices represented on the governing body are heard, it is important to recognise the importance of discussion and deliberation on key strategic issues. Indeed, the most effective governing bodies can be judged by the high quality of their debates and the participation of all their governors. In short, governance is a deliberative process where the different voices come to shared agreements and decisions that are relevant and appropriate.

As we shall show in the following chapters, effective governing bodies deal efficiently with the business and put their energies into strategic interventions, but this should not be at the expense of adequate discussion and debate where the views and concerns of all are taken into account. Just as elected members of the local authority have a duty to promote the well-being of the local community and ensure the delivery of "best value"* public services, so school governors must ensure that their strategic role in raising standards in schools is always interpreted as being in the best interests of the public they represent.

The role of the individual

2

Working in a joined-up way

"What needs to change in schools is how people work, not how much they work. The structures that have separated schools from their surrounding community have made the work more difficult."

M. Fullan and A. Hargreaves, *What's Worth Fighting for out There?*, Teachers College Press, 1998

Being able to see the connections between the different jobs that we do is vital. Unless a governing body can make the relevant links between different items on the agenda for a meeting, between one meeting and the next and between what it is doing and the rest of what is going on in the school, it can be hard for it to get a sense of purpose or achievement. This can lead to disillusionment, on the part of the headteacher as well as the governors, and it militates against fruitful discussion about progress.

Unfortunately, one of the difficulties that has resulted from the incremental build-up of governing body responsibilities is that many governors have found it difficult to get an overview of what they are doing and what their responsibilities amount to. As a result they approach the job as a series of discrete tasks. This disjointed approach to governing body responsibilities tends to obscure what the purpose and role of the governing body are.

To start making sense of the governing body's business, we need to go back to the three key roles, as discussed in the previous chapter. To remind you, they are:

Filling in the three key roles

- setting the school's strategic direction

- being a critical friend – monitoring, evaluating, challenging and supporting

- securing accountability.

One or more of these roles dominates at any given point in the annual work cycle as you exercise responsibility for the "overall management of the school" (*Schools: achieving success*, White Paper of 2001). This work forms a cycle, which can be expressed in the diagram on the next page.

The following details will help put flesh on the bones of these roles. They have been taken from the report of a group convened by the then DfES to look at governor responsibilities.

Setting the school's strategic direction includes:

- determining the school's mission and ethos in the context of developing a strategy for longer-term development

- approving each year the School Development Plan, its targets and the allied budget plan, and making links between them. This should reflect the school's longer-term strategy.

- setting policies on matters such as performance management, recruitment and development of staff, pay, curriculum, organisation of the school and, where appropriate, admissions. You should make sure that these are consonant with each other and with the overall strategy

- appointing the headteacher.

Monitoring and evaluation includes:

- evaluating the school's performance against past performance, against other similar schools, and in the context of its operating environment

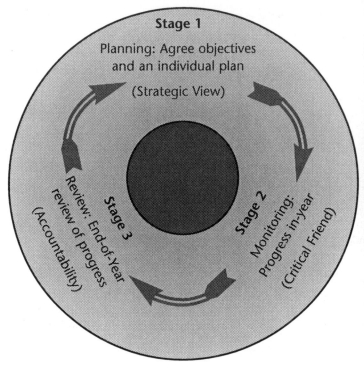

The annual work cycle

- monitoring progress against the approved budget plan and targets

- reviewing and revising policies and plans.

Securing accountability includes:

- reporting to parents, the community and the local authority (LA) on performance and plans against the targets set, including reporting on key developments

- providing information to parents, the community, the LA, DCSF and other government agencies

- hearing appeals, especially on pupil exclusions or staff dismissal, according to grievance procedures

- dealing with general complaints

- for schools with trustees, ensuring compliance with the trust deeds

- decisions on the salary range of the headteacher, and conducting the head's appraisal

- deciding if necessary on the suspension or dismissal of the headteacher

- taking decisions outside established policies.

Key tasks

There are some key tasks around which the governing body business must focus and between which the links must be made. They include:

- *one meeting a year for a formal review of the standards of achievement*

- *identifying the aspects of the school's life which most contribute to the maintenance of standards and those which could help to raise standards further*

- *defining and publishing performance indicators and success criteria; for example, pupil performance targets and results, music and drama productions, sporting achievements, community service activities, parental expressions of satisfaction*

- *ensuring that the National and basic Curriculums are taught and reporting on assessment results and inspections*

- *drawing up a School Development Plan and monitoring its implementation*

- *deciding how to use the school's budget to the best advantage*

- *selecting the head and deputy*

- *on information and advice from the head, promoting and supporting other staff, and ensuring that the senior leadership promotes and itself enjoys a good work-life balance*

- *ensuring that the school strives to meet the Five Outcomes of Every Child Matters*

- *overseeing the provision of extended services in accordance with the needs of the pupils and local community*

- *acting as a link with the parents and local community.*

Making use of the strategic levers Being familiar with the roles would not be of practical use unless you also had the means of carrying them out. In fact, as a governing body you have a number of strategic levers in your hands with which to do this: **planning, allocating resources** and **appraisal**. When they are exercised in the right combinations these levers can bring about major change. Moreover, there are various tools to use in conjunction with each of them, the principal ones of which are, respectively: the School Development Plan (SDP), the budget and the performance management targets and review (particularly of the head, but of all the staff indirectly through the performance management policy, which you agree and monitor).

The overarching responsibility of the governing body is to keep the school developing in the context of a continually changing society. You cannot just wind up a school once and expect it to run perfectly or without stopping! In this state of constant change, schools need to use the strategic levers to make frequent adjustments. For example, we know all too well that members of staff do not stay forever. Each vacancy is an opportunity to consider doing something strategic by reflecting on whether the job description should be changed and what kind of person the school needs now.

School and community in partnership The governing body is strategically placed as it combines members from within the school with those from the community outside. It can therefore bring the needs of the community into the school and take the school out in to the community. The governing body works in partnership with parents, teachers and the head so that the school can do its best by every student. The diagram on the next page illustrates how these partners share this responsibility. It emphasises how at the very heart of the school are the pupils for whom governors and staff together are trying to maintain and, where necessary, improve the standards of educational achievement.

Children do not come to us hermetically sealed but bring with them a whole set of family relationships. These are of

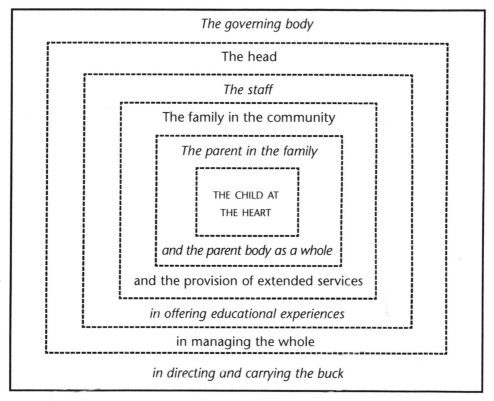

The governing body

The head

The staff

The family in the community

The parent in the family

THE CHILD AT
THE HEART

and the parent body as a whole

and the provision of extended services

in offering educational experiences

in managing the whole

in directing and carrying the buck

(Tom Hinds and Ann Holt, *The New School Governor*, Kogan Page, 1996, adapted)

more immediate influence than the teacher. The teacher then has to take account of what every child brings into the classroom and incorporate this into the teaching and learning process.

The staff and pupils together are the essential components of the school as a place of teaching and learning, whereas the head and governing body work at more of a distance, managing and organising the whole. In the diagram the governing body is deliberately inside the school as it is part of the school as an organisation, but it is close to the boundary with the community because it brings the community into the school and takes the school into the community.

> When asked why she valued her governors one headteacher replied, "They give me the place, space and opportunity to think. In my preparation for the meetings and as I write my report I have to stop, stand back and think. If I didn't have to do it I would become obsessed with the day-to-day operational detail and the school would start to suffer. Of course, this becomes even more valuable if we continue that thinking process in the governors' meetings and spend more time on the future than the past or even the present."

The governing body itself is the place where all the partners who legitimately represent the best interests of the young people meet to do the strategic thinking that is so vital to their success. The governing body needs to be a place to think in, and that means taking the time to do it rather than launching into a series of unrelated tasks. This is not idle contemplation! In order to think strategically you need to know beforehand what the key issues are so that you can reflect, perhaps consult others, and come to the meeting ready to discuss them. This is why the agenda has to be sent out well in advance.

Above all the governing body must make sure that it has time to think strategically. Because if the governing body does not do it, nobody else is going to.

The change equation

The process of achieving successful change or improvement can be expressed in a simple equation:

| VISION + | SKILLS + | INCENTIVES + | RESOURCES + | ACTION PLANS = | CHANGE |

We can concentrate as much as we like on individual components, but we need to have all of them to make real progress. If one of the components is missing then the desired change will not occur.

It is just the same as other equations; $2+3+4+5=14$ does not work if you take out one of the figures. Here, too, if we miss out a component we get a different answer, as shown at the top of the next page:

To change the metaphor, think of cooking from a recipe. One ingredient missing will produce quite a different dish

	SKILLS +	INCENTIVES +	RESOURCES +	ACTION PLANS =	CONFU-SION
VISION +		INCENTIVES +	RESOURCES +	ACTION PLANS =	ANXIETY
VISION +	SKILLS +		RESOURCES +	ACTION PLANS =	GRADUAL CHANGE
VISION +	SKILLS +	INCENTIVES +		ACTION PLANS =	FRUSTRA-TION
VISION +	SKILLS +	INCENTIVES +	RESOURCES =		FALSE STARTS

from the one intended. Creating conditions where the ingredients are all present is the responsibility of the governing body. Making sure that they are properly mixed so that the recipe works is a management responsibility and rests largely in the hands of the headteacher and their team.

We will look at each constituent of the equation in turn.

1. Vision – Establishing a vision and values

To be able to steer firmly to an agreed course, it is essential to have a vision and values. Indeed, the vision and values of a school are what help to define it. They give a school roots. This is essential in a state of change if the school is not to be blown around by transient forces, but having a vision is also about having a language for the future, being able to see where you are going. The governing body has been described as "an expression of the school's organisational values in their largest form, particularly vision and ethics" (John Carver, *Boards That Make a Difference*, Jossey-Bass, San Francisco, 1997). Put more simply, the governing body is there to help "decide what it is good and wise to be doing" (*ibid.*).

In *Schools: achieving success* the government stated the importance of creating schools "with character". It talked about every school being good at all the basics and excellent at much more, and every school having a distinct mission, ethos and character. The government's ambition is that every school should be able to define how it wants to be special. Whether this happens within the context of seeking specialist status or not, or becoming a trust school or not, the governing body is the forum in which to identify the aims that will make the school distinctive.

Putting the vision and aims into practice

As we have seen, it is the responsibility of the governors to discuss, define and articulate the vision for the school's future. The vision must be based on shared values and beliefs and should provide the principles behind decision-making and action. Most schools now have a mission statement in which they try to encapsulate the vision, but drawing it up will have been an empty exercise if it does little more than grace the wall of the entrance hall and is never actually used. We are talking about more than a slogan here. What is required is a touchstone by which the intention and effectiveness of actions can be tested.

The mission statement is meant to guide you in defining and setting aims and objectives. It is the component that binds the others together. The problems in many schools, and the reason why they can feel that they are sinking in a sea of initiatives, is that, in the words of a Chief Inspector of Schools, they "are awash with dislocated targets". Not linking the targets together is a recipe for losing them, which makes the whole exercise of setting them pointless. It is therefore vital that wherever objectives or targets are being set they are aligned to the same priorities and governed by the same vision and values.

There are three key points in the work cycle of governing bodies at which it becomes essential for you to get the process of alignment right:

1.when drawing up the School Development Plan, within which the *whole organisation targets* will be defined

2.when discussing and agreeing to *pupil performance targets* each year

3.when agreeing the headteacher's *performance objectives* for the year.

All of these should be linked to one another to make sure that they contribute to achieving the overall vision. A robust performance management system links some of the strategic and operational responsibilities of the governing body. When governors are involved in school development planning and pupil performance target-setting they are acting strategically. The same is true when they establish the performance management policy for the school. Other aspects of the governing body's role also link into these tasks, as the governing body monitors progress and ensures accountability on these matters. And some of the work that some members of the governing body do that appears to be more operational is in fact a function of these responsibilities.

A robust performance management system can only operate if there is a clearly defined plan which outlines objectives for the school. Most schools have a strategic plan, mission statement and operational ethos that are reflected in the values, aims and targets (output) to be achieved at clearly defined dates in the year(s) ahead. This is the context in which the objectives for the head and other staff should be agreed. To do so will ensure that all are focused on the development of the school, and that the SDP leads to the desired outcomes in both pupil and staff performance.

These three points make up a triangle, which can be seen as the model of joined-up governance, as illustrated in the diagram overleaf.

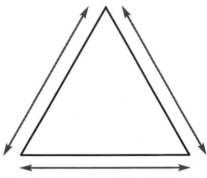

School Development Plan

Teacher Objectives   Pupil Outcomes (Targets)

The joined-up governance model

The targets at any point on the triangle should inform the objectives at any of the other points. Among the performance management objectives for every member of the teaching and management staff have to be ones linked to pupil performance. The targets in the SDP will identify how the organisation as a whole needs to change its priorities in order to achieve better pupil performance.

More will be said about the practicalities of target-setting in the next chapter on planning, policy-making and decision-making. What needs to be said here is that the aims and values are not merely for the long term but should inform decisions about the immediate future, and that will affect long-term outcomes and achievements. In turn, decisions about resourcing, development and rewards should be made to underpin decisions about what needs to be improved and achieved and reflect the values that are embraced in the vision. For example, schools that aim to enable every child to reach their potential (a frequently used phrase) must have resourcing policies that reflect this.

In short, the three functions of the aims and vision can be described as follows:

- to inspire

- to be the cornerstone for decision-making

- to align everyone's energies within the organisation.

In terms of our change equation, without a vision you will not head for change but for *confusion*.

2. Skills – Acquiring and developing the skills to realise the vision

If you were an artist and you had a mental picture of a painting you wanted to produce, you would first have to make sure that you had got the paints, brushes and canvas with which to make this vision concrete. In schools, the means of realising the vision are much more subtle and exciting – they are people.

There is no doubt that after the pupils the most important element of school is the staff: those who manage, those who teach and those who act as support. They are also an important set of voices on the governing body, and the rest of the governors need to listen carefully to their views about their capacity to achieve the vision. Without the necessary talent and skill, instead of change you will create *anxiety* among the staff, and that leads to stress.

Making appointments

It can be argued that the most important responsibilities that a governing body carries are to do with the appointing, valuing and developing of the staff. In voluntary aided and foundation schools the governing body is the staff employer; in community and voluntary controlled schools the employer is legally the LA but most of the employer responsibilities are delegated to the governors. Of course, as the key manager, the headteacher will advise the governing body on the best staffing structure and the right skills mix.

The appointment of a new head, which is arguably the most significant appointment in the school, has always to be in the hands of the governors. This also applies to the appointment of a deputy. When it comes to appointing other staff, although legally the responsibility is the governing body's, guidance from the DCSF states that this responsibility should be delegated to the headteacher. However, particularly in primary schools, the headteacher often wants governors to be involved, and a selection panel will be formed of a number of governors, the headteacher and/or another senior member of staff.

When looking for staff it is important that the vision is clear and the needs have been carefully identified, even when you have delegated the appointments process. Interviews will lack clarity if you know only that you have to appoint a member of the senior team but do not understand the precise nature of your needs. It will usually guarantee that you will fail to make the appointment that meets your strategy.

However, in reality few staff match perfectly the ideal that has been put in the job description and person specification, so you may have to make adjustments to your expectations as you go along. Everyone is likely to come to the interview with talents other than those that have been identified in advance, and these should be brought out. What is more, jobs change and people grow. In employment generally there is greater emphasis these days on flexibility and building jobs around people's identified talents. Teaching is no exception.

Staff development
Staffing responsibilities do not end when an appointment is made. We should satisfy ourselves that appropriate welcoming and induction procedures are in place for new staff and that ongoing support is provided for all staff. Retaining teachers is as important as recruiting new ones, especially in times of staff shortages.

In fact, the government places considerable emphasis on continuing professional development, with nationally validated programmes and grants to schools to fund them. They are also very keen for schools to share their talented teachers with others by becoming training schools or by collaborating with each other. Any responsible governing body will want to make the most of it staff and to develop them. All teachers have to be change agents, and to succeed in this they have to grow and change themselves.

This is where performance management fits into the picture. The responsibility that governors have for this is central to the development of the school. Systematic reviews that enable teachers and their managers to identify the teachers' strengths and weaknesses are crucial. When taken in the overview such information will give you and the head a strong indication of what skills can be developed within the existing staff and where there are gaps that need to be filled.

It is worth bearing in mind here that research has shown that training and development achieve the best results when they are used to play to peoples' strengths rather than trying to make up for their deficiencies. These are best dealt with by working round them. It is said that the champion golfer, Tiger Woods, is not so good at getting out of bunkers and so his trainer works on his drive to stop him getting into them. Unfortunately most of us get into the equivalent of a bunker from time to time, and that is where, unlike Tiger Woods, the talents of the rest of the team come in to help us get out! This is the advantage of teamwork: there will be someone else whose speciality is the very thing that you are weak at.

When looking at the allocation of finance to staffing it is important not to fall into the temptation of increasing the number of staff at the expense of developing the ones you already have. The Standards Fund* devolved to schools includes what can amount to a considerable sum of money for continuing professional development. The governing body has the same responsibility for making sure that these funds are used to match strategic priorities as it does over any other resources.

Asterisked terms are defined in the Glossary, pages 116–21

3. Incentives

One of the problems facing schools is that of morale and motivation. Having got the best staff we can, how do we encourage them and keep them motivated? For without motivation, progress will be at best *gradual* or sluggish, and may not be achieved at all.

The incentives available to governors range from the simple

thank-you to financial rewards and promotion. Money is clearly important, but it is not the only incentive, or even the most important one. When some teachers were asked what kept them going they stressed two things: being appreciated and having the ability to influence and have some control over what is happening in their school.

Appreciation costs little but it is so easy to overlook. The note that lets someone know that you have noticed their efforts and achievement can be a real encouragement, as can the governors hosting a celebration for the whole staff. We also have a significant part to play in praising the school in public and to parents when it is deserved.

The staff of the school feel more secure and therefore more in control when they sense that the school's leadership knows where it is going and what it wants done. They want to know that the governors and the head have a grip on things and are able to keep that strategic overview, which in turn will help the managers and teachers to get on top of the detail.

Governors now have specific additional responsibility for the welfare of school staff. As a consequence of the National Workforce Agreement signed in January 2003 by most of the teaching unions and the government all teachers are now entitled to have 10 percent of their timetabled time set aside for planning, preparation and assessment (PPA). This was designed to stop them having to perform these tasks in their own time, and is a part of the drive to enable teachers to achieve a healthy work-life balance. As well as ensuring that teachers get the 10 percent PPA time, governors are meant to check with the school management that other measures are in place if necessary to give teachers a good work-life balance, and should themselves give the headteacher the same benefit.

It is the responsibility of government to set before us a standard for what is needed to compete nationally and internationally, and it is the responsibility of the LA to help us to benchmark* locally. But the responsibility for the progress of the children in a particular school and the performance of the staff remains the business of the school. The pupil performance targets and the performance management objectives have therefore been placed in the hands of those who know the local factors well, namely the governors and staff of the school. These are the people who are in control at school level. The governing body gives its consent to matters that are the concern of the local interest groups and then they must protect what they have consented to. For example, each year it is up to the governing body to consent to the pupil performance targets and then to defend those targets if they are challenged by the LA or a parent. When staff are supported in this way their morale is higher.

Incentives and skills are also closely linked. Again, the staff will be more highly motivated if they know that you are funding and supporting a properly thought-through continuing professional development programme, providing that it is fair to all and linked to the review and objectives identified within the performance management programme. You will not be involved in the detailed implementation of this, but you should expect regular reports from the head about the achievements, development and wellbeing of the staff, and how they are serving the process of school improvement. These are vital if you are going to monitor the performance management policy and its impact, as indeed you must. Regulations require heads to report to the whole governing body on performance matters. You, in turn should ensure that your own decisions link to what you have agreed to as desirable outcomes of performance, and evaluate the impact of your own actions.

4. Resources – Using them effectively

The vast proportion of the local authority schools' budget is in the hands of schools. But where the resources are insufficient or badly deployed then instead of progress or change you get *frustration*.

Despite the increase in funds in recent years, the amounts given to schools are not generous and still require careful stewardship. Furthermore, the funding does not all come in one pot, nor is all the extra funding available to all schools. In the secondary sector in particular, some of the additional monies available are linked to specialist status in, say, languages or technology or specific achievement. In the inner cities there is more money available linked to the Excellence in Cities Programme*. The granting of such funds depends on the school making a case for them, and that in turn calls for a sense of purpose and clear strategic thinking. The governing body is the normal arena for such thinking.

Seeking special status In pursuing any form of special status you should remember that planning should not be finance-led. The reasons for a particular initiative in a school must be educational and about enhanced learning, and if it appears that your motives are purely financial you are unlikely to be awarded the status. However, finance is a powerful strategic lever when it comes to moving plans forward.

Staff pay Since staffing takes at least 85 per cent of the budget in most schools, it is crucial that the expenditure on this item is carefully monitored. One school was found to be spending 92 per cent of its budget on salaries because over the years vacancies had been filled without any thought as to whether the old staffing structure and staff levels were still appropriate. Consequently, the school never had enough money for incentives, either by way of staff development or promotion.

You now have a considerable range of ways of increasing the pay of individuals. There are various pay discretions that have been made available to governors. However, decisions should not be made piecemeal, but in the context of your school's pay policy. In considering these discretions, you can use information from the performance review statements, in the following ways:

- Up to threshold* (i.e. up to the highest point on the

teachers' pay scale*) teachers can expect an annual increment if their performance is satisfactory. Double increments may be awarded for exceptional performance evidenced by a performance review.

- Teachers who have reached the threshold and want to move to the upper pay spine have to apply by filling out an application form. They are assessed by their headteacher, using evidence from performance reviews. If the head decides they should be moved across the threshold, the headteacher asks the governing body to do so.

Performance also forms part of the evidence where schools are considering:

- moving post-threshold teachers up to Excellent Teacher* status

- moving a teacher to a Teaching and Learning Responsibility* position, where they will have some management responsibilities

- recommending that a teacher become an advanced skills teacher*. This provides opportunities for teachers demonstrating excellent practice in the classroom to share their skills and experience with others.

Planning your spending

It is usual for the governing body to give the head and senior management team a fair amount of discretion over spending, within defined boundaries that are linked to the school's priorities. When a major investment is to be made, such as in technology or a new reading scheme, this should be discussed at governor level (either full governing body or finance committee). You have the power to authorise the spending, but it would be impertinent to make the decisions about which computers or which reading scheme. That is for the professionals to decide. It is appropriate, however, for you to want to know how effective such an investment has been when it comes to judging progress. That is part of the joined-up thinking!

Aligning the budget to the SDP The reason for setting a budget linked to the SDP is to ensure that resources are targeted efficiently and effectively to maintain the quality of education provided and improve standards. Budgeting is not just about balancing the books.

Some governing bodies use uncertainties about future levels of funding as a reason for not taking a longer-term view of budget setting, but in reality this is one of the reasons for adopting a more strategic view in financial management.

Budgeting becomes linked to development planning when you ask these sorts of question:

- What do we need to do to raise the quality of our educational provision?

- What is our financial provision?

- What do we need to spend this year and in the future?

- What are our options?

- What will the budget look like this year and next year?

The Dedicated School Grant, the Standards Fund* and the School Standards Grant have given governing bodies considerable control over expenditure and more money (though government has also found extra things they have to spend it on), and greater autonomy for schools is meant to grant even more control.

5. Planning for action

The final element in the change equation is no less vital than the others. Any changes need a well-drawn-up plan to secure the improvements desired. Indeed, Ofsted used to recognise the importance of action planning by insisting that each school drew up an action plan after inspection to address weaknesses. This is now only a statutory requirement of schools judged to be failing, but it is expected that other schools will realise they need to plan appropriately.

Good action plans should identify:

- the actions to be taken or the tasks set

- the people responsible

- the dates for the start and completion of the action

- the resources and costs involved

- the success criteria

- who is to monitor the implementation

- who is to evaluate the effect, and how they will do this.
(*Making it Better*, Ofsted, 2001)

Without properly thought-out action plans your initiatives are likely to lead to a series of *false starts*.

The agenda as a working tool

The meetings and discussions of the governing body are likely to be governed by how well prepared they are, and the agenda can be a great help here. When the clerk, the chair and the head are preparing it they are in fact leading the governing body in what needs to be done. The aim must always be to concentrate on its key function:

"The aim of the Government is to ensure that all children have the best possible education, tailored to their needs, interests and aptitudes. Governing bodies are central to achieving this aim."

Foreword to *Governing the School of the Future*, DfES, 2004

Chapter 4, Getting Down to Business, says more about this. It is just sufficient to note here that items on the agenda should be linked to each other, should link with other governing body meetings and committees, and should link with the other monitoring activities. As we have seen, a good agenda will make it clear where the strategic thinking is to be done and where there is need for reflection.

Taking risks

Finally, bear in mind that among the most successful schools are those that are prepared to take risks, because the pace of change requires some risky living. The Coverdale School of Management says "It is better to ask for forgiveness than permission!" The forward-looking governing body will create a climate in which staff are encouraged "to go for it" but to admit if things are going wrong so that the governing body can then join forces with them to solve the problems. In too many governing bodies it feels as though difficult issues are covered up rather than confronted. In adversity many governors either behave as though they don't want to know or come down like a ton of bricks on someone they can blame. Where either response is typical, heads try to avoid telling the governors anything that might be construed as bad news, and as a consequence any notion of accountability goes out of the window.

It is vital that governors and heads establish a feeling of being in things together. Then we all have available a collective wisdom, gleaned from both the internal and external perspectives. That way we will together be creating a learning community in which:

- "the total brainpower of the organisation is released

- there is a sense of ethos built on enduring values

- new opportunities are created

- there is an environment that embraces and manages change."

Tom Bentley, director of DEMOS

That way we shall have created a school that is not overwhelmed, feeling itself to the victim of pressures from elsewhere, but is in control of where it is going – one that has a clear view of what is good for its pupils.

Making governance work — the policy-making and planning processes   3

"It should not be up to the CEO (the head) to make sure that the board conducts itself responsibly. But as we know, a board frequently sends a confusing message to their CEO. 'You work for us, now tell us what to do.'"

    John Carver, *The CEO Role under Policy Governance*,
Jossey-Bass, San Francisco, 1997

Clarifying the role of the head

When it comes to describing how governance works at a strategic level, John Carver, an American expert on the governance of educational organisations, uses the image of an egg timer to help us picture the relationship between the governing body, the headteacher and the staff. The headteacher is in the narrow part of the funnel. Above is the governing body, determining the expectations and the character of the school. Below is the staff, all with different job descriptions, working to fulfil those expectations. The headteacher is at the point in the decision-making where the flow of authority downward and accountability upwards go through a single human being. No wonder headteachers sometimes feel squeezed!

As was described in chapter 1, some tasks are solely in the head's domain, some can only be done by the governing body, and some can be delegated by the governing body. → pages 23–5

However, the extent of delegation cannot be decided, nor can the jobs of head and staff be properly defined, until the governing body has stated what it expects in the way of achievement and progress towards school improvement. This is its strategic role. The governing body is ultimately accountable for an institution in which a multitude of tasks that it does not see are undertaken daily. To fulfil such a responsibility it must charge the head with a job that is clear and which comes with an unambiguous authority to make decisions according to agreed expectations and direction.

Directions are no good unless they are clear and communicated effectively. If the governing body is unclear about its expectations and how to communicate them, the channel between it and the staff will become blocked. It follows then that the governing body must establish and adhere to the principles of good communication.

Communicate, communicate

All governors should work at communication but the chair, the head and the clerk have particular responsibilities in this area.

The chair is responsible for orchestrating the meetings and making sure that everyone has an opportunity to contribute. In addition, the chair has a public relations role and will have to communicate with parents, the LA and, from time to time, the press. The chair is also likely to be in more regular communication with the head than any of the other governors.

The head is responsible for the day-to-day management of the school. The head is also responsible for communicating essential developments and issues to the governing body. Many heads are governors, but all heads, whether governors or not, must function as chief executives to governing bodies. This is a statutory part of their role.

The clerk to the governors cannot be a governor and has to be specially appointed. He or she is responsible for communications between meetings and for ensuring that meetings are properly convened so that everyone knows what is happening. Some clerks minute the meetings; others adopt a more advisory role but ensure that accurate minutes are taken. Many clerks are very knowledgeable and are well equipped to offer procedural advice; if your clerk is not qualified to offer such advice, they should know where to get it.

Most governors are not educational professionals, but that does not mean that governance should be conducted in an amateurish way. You would not expect a St John's Ambulance Brigade volunteer to be a qualified doctor, but it would be bad news if they did not know how to do first aid correctly! Similarly, volunteer governors must learn the art of proper governance, and communication is one of the keys.

Communication is not just a matter of informing the parents what you are doing. It is about how the governing body relates to itself, to ensure that important issues are identified, discussed as fully as needed, and responded to with decisions that arise from informed consideration.

Some of the key principles of good communication are:

• Communication should be open.

• Everyone should be honest.

• Conflict should be used constructively.

• Issues should be confronted, not ducked.

• Feelings should be acknowledged.

• Confidentiality should be respected.

These principles apply to every situation in which you find yourself as a governor, whether you are in a meeting or holding a conversation.

Communication is in part about getting yourself heard. In meetings there is an art to getting attention paid to your contribution. This involves:

- explaining your own feelings

- referring back to points that others have made

- making your own points in a firm but friendly manner.

Then we need to listen actively to others by showing that we understand:

- that they feel strongly

- what they feel strongly about

- and why they feel that way.

The good communicator works to a joint solution by

- seeking the ideas of others

- building on their ideas

- offering their own ideas

- constructing the solution from everyone's contribution.

Planning Having understood the principles of good communication, the governing body must attend to some key processes.

In order to achieve anything you need to translate the joined-up model discussed in the last chapter into practice by following the basic management cycle of planning, monitoring and review.

→ page 32

The first stage, and the one that relates most closely to the governors' strategic role, is planning. In order to plan where the school should go the governing body needs to know where the school currently is in terms of school improvement. Researchers Louise Stoll and Dean Fink (*Changing Our Schools*, 1996) coined five basic descriptions, any one of which will apply to a school at any particular time. Before you start making detailed plans, you need to know which of these descriptions most fits your school. These are: the *moving* school, the *coasting* school, the *strolling* school, the *struggling* school and the *sinking* school.

The five states

The moving school:

- boosts pupil progress
- responds to change and keeps developing
- knows where it wants to go
- has the will and skills to get there.

The coasting school:

- appears to be effective
- may have high test scores
- has achieving pupils even if there is some poor teaching
- does not prepare its students for the changing world.

The strolling school:

- moves too slowly to cope with the pace of change
- has ill-defined and conflicting aims that inhibit progress.

The struggling school:

- knows that it is ineffective
- expends considerable energy to improve
- is willing to try anything
- finds some of its efforts are unproductive
- will ultimately succeed.

The sinking school:

- is ineffective
- is isolated and too self-reliant
- has staff that seem unable to change
- has a culture of blaming others
- needs dramatic action and significant support.

Adapted from L. Stoll and D. Fink, *Changing Our Schools*, Open University Press, 1996

The following diagram is a kind of map on which you can place your school. It is important to note that the struggling school lies on the improving side because, like the struggling swimmer, all is not yet lost! While you are struggling you have not drowned. On the other hand, the coasting school may look successful but it will be in danger of losing momentum and then starting to ship water.

	IMPROVING	DECLINING
EFFECTIVE	Moving	Coasting
	Strolling	
INEFFECTIVE	Struggling	Sinking

When you have got a rough idea of where you think your school is there are various tools that can be used to analyse what the reasons for its position may be. You may well be familiar with the SWOT* analysis, in which people work in groups to list the strengths and weaknesses of their organisation, and the opportunities and threats facing it. Carrying out this exercise in your governing body will take some time, a couple of hours at least, and requires a certain amount of data, such as the staffing profile or levels of pupil attainment, but can be an excellent use of a special governing body meeting. Most people find listing the internal strengths and weaknesses easy, but the opportunities and threats are usually more difficult to identify because they may come as a result of external factors. An additional tool can help with this: the STEEPE analysis.

Asterisked terms are defined in the Glossary, pages 116–21

STEEPE analysis A STEEPE analysis asks you to list under various headings what is happening on the wider scene that affects your school. These headings are given below, together with examples taken from a real-life situation experienced by a rural secondary school in the summer of 2001. These are intended to clarify what is meant by each of the terms.

Social   e.g. a changed social mix in the area

Technological e.g. introduction of a new computer application

Environmental e.g. the outbreak of foot and mouth disease

Economic   e.g. the closure of a local source of employment

Political   e.g. a change of government

Educational   e.g. new targets for 14–19-year-olds

Could you list something under one of these headings that is significant for your school and which originates outside it, either in a national trend or more local events? Then look at why it is significant for your school. Does it present an opportunity, or does it represent a threat? In either case, it is not an option to ignore it; you have to take the analysis into the planning and problem-solving processes.

For the school shown in the examples it was only when the governing body started to use this tool that it got down to thinking about the impact of the closure of a large local firm and the opening of a branch of a multinational company in their area. It realised that over the following five years there would be a huge change in the types of job on offer and that this could change the family and pupil profile within the school's catchment area. This in turn could affect the staffing needs of the school.

Tools like SWOT and STEEPE analyses help us engage in an internal and external audit of what's going on. But they are not the only analyses you will be making during the conduct of governing body business. Others that will also influence the decisions about the eventual priorities include:

• an audit of staffing needs

• a review of staff deployment and performance

- a review of the curriculum
- a review of pupil performance
- a best value analysis of spending
- an accommodation audit
- a survey of pupil/parent satisfaction and demand
- comparative measures of the school's overall performance.

Most governing bodies are used to acquiring this sort of data, but it is one thing having it and another making use of it. To do this it has to be questioned and turned into real information. The critical friend role comes to the fore here. You will remember that one of the key functions of the governing body is to ask critical questions – in a sensitive manner.

When it comes to testing assumptions in a spirit of critical friendship the principles of best value are good ones to adopt. These invite us to question our intentions and decisions under four headings, commonly known as "the four Cs":

- compare
- challenge
- consult
- compete.

When making *comparisons*, you need to know what the quality of education provided by similar schools is; how the standards compare with your school's; whether the school is a relatively high or low performer, and whether it is spending more than other schools on the same things. Valuable information for making comparisons is supplied each year in the autumn in RAISEonline to help schools benchmark themselves against national performance, while your LA will supply local benchmarking data. It is the role of the head and LA advisers to provide governors, if asked, with a professional commentary on this data.

The governing body needs to *challenge* itself and others with questions such as "Why are we doing this?" "What is the evidence of the level of need?" "Is it what the parents and pupils want?" "Could we or someone else do it differently or better?"

In terms of the third "c", *"consult"*, you will always get a better understanding of what needs to be done when making major changes if you talk to all the parties concerned – resist the temptation heroically to go it alone.

When it comes to *competitiveness*, the school must try to ensure that it receives and gives the most effective, efficient and economic service – a service that adds real value to what the pupils can achieve.

Of course, you would not do a full-scale audit every time you were faced with drawing up a plan for some aspect of the school's activity, but this is a valuable exercise to do once a year. And once performed, the elements of the audit become part of your thinking processes, so that, for example, the four Cs of best value come to mind when making any resourcing decision.

With the internal and external audits behind you, it is time to start planning for improvement, and that will mean changes. It is never appropriate to stand still; remember, you don't have to be poorly to get better.

Refer back to the diagram of the management cycle. The evaluation of the information gathered at the monitoring and review stages of the cycle will begin to answer the question "How good a school are we?". You will also need to return to the vision that you have corporately determined for your school to see how you are matching up. To do this you should have established some overall performance indicators and some success criteria for your great expectations.

It will help if you have some idea of what your school will look like if you achieve your vision. When once you have formulated the visions, the idea is to create a strategic plan

Planning for school improvement

→ page 32

> ## Vision of a successful school
>
> *One governing body and staff together came up with the following characteristics:*
>
> > *a disciplined, civilised environment*
> > *no fear*
> > *a good work ethic*
> > *children who achieve their potential*
> > *individuals are cared for*
> > *there is stability*
> > *there is a sense of community*
> > *beliefs and values are made explicit*
> > *expectations are high*
> > *the weak are encouraged*
> > *there is praise for the successful*
> > *there is reconciliation and forgiveness*
> > *there is celebration and laughter*
> > *everyone has hope.*

from which to bring it about. The aims of your plan will be about achieving the right mixture of success factors, many of which are dependent upon one another. For example, a disciplined and civilised environment is one in which children are likely to achieve their potential. Equally a sense of community helps to breed stability.

The School Development Plan

Usually called the School Development Plan (SDP) and sometimes the School Improvement Plan (SIP) or the School Development Plan for Improvement, this document is the most obvious product of the planning process. But to have arrived at a plan is not the end of the matter; it is only the beginning. The idea is that the plan specifies the priorities to be addressed by the school and the strategies to be employed over three or so years. It is likely that there will be a degree of interdependence between some of the objectives, and you should be aware of these connections when you do your own thinking.

The final result of the outcomes defined in the plan must be pupil progress and therefore, as explained in chapter 2, the plan must be married up with pupil performance targets. → page 39 The selection of priorities should show a balance between what needs to be maintained (areas of excellence) and what needs to be changed. They should incorporate local and national priorities and lead to a clear plan of action.

In many schools the head does much of the preliminary work on the SDP. The plan is then presented to the governing body in a complete form, to be approved or amended. However, there are dangers if the head goes too far before consulting anyone. For a plan to be effective it needs to be owned by those who have to implement it and those who have to agree it. It is essential that staff and governors are involved in the planning process.

Many schools are beginning to devote serious resources to the planning process. Every three years they convene a working party made up of senior managers, governors and staff to do sustained strategic thinking in order to come up with a new development plan. Each year they will devote one of their development days to review and revision, and will invite governors to join them. This kind of attention is likely to produce a corporate plan that is useful to everyone.

The plan should be a working document that informs all levels of management decision-making. However, it should not be regarded as being written on tablets of stone. While the priorities that have been carefully identified should not be easily displaced, adjustments could be made to respond to changing circumstances.

The governing body is charged with setting targets of pupil performance. The targets set in the planning stage of the cycle help to define what you are aiming for and are vital for later monitoring and evaluation.

Pupil performance targets

The governing body has to agree the school's pupil performance targets for each year. We do not have to draw them up, as that requires detailed knowledge of the pupils, which is in the teachers' domain. The headteacher proposes targets for the governing body to approve. In doing that we have to ask whether they are realistic and appropriate. This much is common sense, but to make the assessment as to whether they are appropriate we need to ask questions. The sorts of questions we should be asking ourselves and the head should be along the lines of:

1. How did the school perform last year in particular curriculum areas?

2. How have pupils performed in relation to their prior attainment, both overall and in identifiable groups such as particular sets, boys and girls, ethnic groups?

3. Are some groups of pupils performing better, and if so, why?

4. How do the school's current achievements compare with previous ones?

5. Are some areas showing a marked improvement or decline?

6. Are there any trends over the past three years that indicate action that needs to be taken by the head and staff?

7. Since every teacher has to have objectives linked to pupil progress, what are the emerging priorities for the school as a whole, and for the different year groups or departments? (These priorities should have found their way in to the SDP. They should also inform the priorities when agreeing headteacher and teacher performance objectives in performance management reviews.)

Target setting

Governing bodies in England have to set targets for pupil performance at the end of Key Stage* 2 (primary schools) and KS3 and 4 (secondary schools). Those for KS2 and 3 are for performance in Standard Assessment Tests*; those in KS 4 are for public examinations. These targets have to be set by the end of December for pupils completing the KS five terms later.

You may also want to ask:

8. Can any particular teaching and learning practices be identified that have contributed to successful outcomes in particular areas?

9. Are any of these features appropriate for consideration by staff across the whole school, particularly where performance is below the national average?

Over the years governors have become more confident in asking questions, but sometimes we need to be a little more probing, without being inquisitional.

Agreeing teacher performance objectives

Once a year the governing body is responsible for agreeing performance objectives for the headteacher. The head and team leaders do this for the rest of the teaching staff. In the case of the headteacher, this has to be done by the end of each calendar year, and forms part of the performance management review. Setting these targets is an important part of the planning process, while assessing during the review how far the head has met the previous year's is a core monitoring activity.

All teachers, including headteachers, must have objectives that link to pupil progress and to their own professional development. In addition, you should agree with the head leadership and management objectives, which are in turn reflected in the SDP – managers should also have such objectives. Again, the power of this activity arises when links are made to the school's priorities for pupil achievement and moving the organisation forward.

SMART criteria

Like all objectives, those you agree with the headteacher should be SMART:

Specific	Relevant
Measurable	Time-related.
Achievable	

When setting objectives the pro-forma to the right will simultaneously help you to apply the SMART criteria and to relate the objectives to the wider context of school improvement. The second column contain questions. Write your answers in the third column, which will then give you the elements of the objective that you need to write.

The balanced scorecard A useful tool for helping with joined-up planning and performance management at whole-school level is the "balanced scorecard". This tool encourages school planners to define goals under four linked headings:

Learning perspective – core purpose of the organisation

Internal perspective – pupils, staff, governing body, etc.

External perspective – parents, employers, etc.

Financial perspective – budget

The balanced scorecard focuses attention on the most critical items and places strategic objectives at the centre of the agenda. It also balances financial measures with other important performance measures.

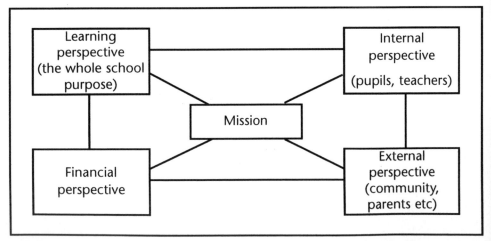

The principle of the balanced scorecard

Pro-forma for setting objectives		
CONTEXT	What is the current situation? Priorities in the SDP Priorities for pupil performance Targets, etc	
OBJECTIVE Outcome	What do we want the head to achieve? Specific improvement/change/development	
clear (range) / Specific ＼ *concise*	Which pupils? Which subject? Which teachers? Which management area?	
monitor / *evidence* Measurable ＼ *result*	(Performance indicator/success criteria) What evidence is required? What is the extent of the expected change?	
challenging/realistic / Achievable ＼ *resources*	Can you do it and how difficult will it be? What else is there already? What else is needed?	
impact / Relevant *context* ＼ *job description*	Is there a core improvement? Does the context suggest this is a priority? Why is this your responsibility?	
review date / Time-related ＼ *milestone*	When should this be reviewed? What interim monitoring dates are appropriate?	

The pro-forma to the right shows how to use this tool. If has been filled in with some sample answers, but a blank version is included at the back of the book, which you can → pages 114–15 photocopy.

Implementing the School Development Plan

The final plan is quite a complex document and is likely to be used for a variety of purposes. Implementation will be dependent upon annual action plans, financial resources and a staff development programme. You should monitor progress systematically and use a range of qualitative and quantitative evidence to evaluate the outcomes. The more robust the planning and self-evaluation processes inside the school the less likely are interferences from outside, as you will have demonstrated that you have a grip on the school's improvement. Indeed, the government has deregulated in recent years and given more autonomy to schools that can demonstrate that they have this grip. Processes such as pupil performance target-setting and teacher performance management may seem like extra work, but they are designed to give governors and managers stronger control and a greater ability to manage change and improvement.

The following checklist of questions will help you to see if your plan is on the right track.

• Does the plan reflect the concerns of all the relevant stakeholders?

• Is the plan focused on developments related to pupil achievements and meeting the Five Outcomes of Every Child Matters*?

• Does the plan contain a realistic number of developments?

• Are the success criteria specific, clear and capable of investigation?

The Five Outcomes

Every Child Matters *stated that there should be five outcomes for children from education, now embodied in the Children Act 2004:*

• *being healthy*

• *staying safe*

• *enjoying and achieving through learning*

• *making a positive contribution to society*

• *achieving economic well-being.*

Balanced scorecard pro-forma

1. Mission

What is it currently? Use your vision, mission and overall aims statements to fill this in.

GOALS	SUCCESS INDICATORS

2. The learning perspective

To become a specialist school in creative arts — *Reputation recognised by successful bid for creative arts and specialist status*

3. The internal perspective

Takes account of the needs of all who learn and work in the school

To set up a writer-in-residence scheme — *Writer working in the school with staff and children*

4. The external perspective

Who are our key interest groups? What do they expect?

To improve relations with a major local employer — *New governor to be co-opted from this source*

To involve more parents in school productions — *Six more parents involved*

5. The financial perspective

What is our budget? Are there other funds to tap into?

To increase sponsorship for enhanced drama facilities — *Money coming in from this source*

How do we do it? Our strategic objectives

1   *Fill the teacher vacancy in English with a drama specialist.*

2   *Set up a working group to develop and implement a sponsorship strategy and specialist status bid to DCSF.*

3   *Set up a writer-in-residence scheme.*

4

5

6

- Does the plan include strategies for monitoring its implementation?

- Are the connections between different aims and actions identified?

Action plans Before we move on to monitoring and evaluation it is necessary to say something about action plans and policies.

Generally governing bodies are much more concerned over what needs to be done and why than they are over how things are to be done, which is largely a professional matter and the concern of the implementers and managers. One writer on the theory of governance, John Carver, has said that governing bodies would be better to set boundaries over which the managers should not go without good reason and then leave them to get on with it.

However, in order to bring the SDP to fruition governing bodies do need to have action plans. Both the SDP and the plans mean some involvement in the "how". You will not be expected to draw these up yourself, as they will be done by the headteacher or senior management. Your involvement in the "how" is there because you need to know the proposed means to achieve the ends you have articulated. Knowing the details of how the plan is to be carried out also helps you → pages 48–9 monitor its implementation.

Policies All schools have a number of policies which govern how they do things as well as why they do them, and the governing body has responsibility for a number of these:

- Sex education

- Pupil behaviour

- Health and safety

- Performance management

- Staff pay

- Admissions (in voluntary aided and foundation schools)

- Charging and remissions.

In addition there can be any number of policies to do with aspects of the curriculum and internal management with which the governing body will not, in the normal course of events, be concerned.

Policies are important because they state how we would normally expect things to be done.

In general they should give the norms that cover a particular sphere of activity. They give a framework for action, and in so doing should provide clarity, protection and continuity. They are also important mechanisms for accountability – for the governing body to hold the staff to account and for parents to hold the governing body to account.

From time to time policies should be reviewed by asking "critical friend" questions such as:

- Are the people responsible for carrying out the polices doing so?

- Are there any problems or difficulties with the policy?

- Has the policy been properly communicated to those who need to understand it?

- Is the policy adequately resourced if it needs funds?

Like plans, policies are about action and not just getting a document to put in a file. It is important that they reflect what the school really does and are not merely documents produced to serve a bureaucratic demand. The pay policy, for example, should reflect the performance management policy, and both should be familiar to those responsible for recruitment, retention and promotion decisions for staff.

Monitoring and evaluation

The school development planning cycle is completed with monitoring, evaluation and reporting. Proper review is a part of the audit process with which we began, and hence is part of the strategic function of the governing body. In contrast, monitoring is an aspect of the critical friend role and evaluation and reporting are a part of accountability, both of which are dealt with more fully in the next two chapters. Nevertheless, they are also parts of the management cycle and of the school development planning cycle, so are looked at here in general terms.

Monitoring progress We started by looking at the planning stage, but in reality planning is *preceded* by monitoring and review every bit as much as it *leads* to them. The information gathered in monitoring will have begun to identify the issues that you need

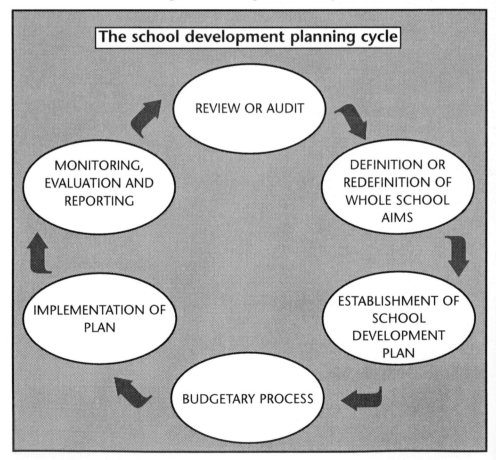

The school development planning cycle

REVIEW OR AUDIT

MONITORING, EVALUATION AND REPORTING

DEFINITION OR REDEFINITION OF WHOLE SCHOOL AIMS

IMPLEMENTATION OF PLAN

ESTABLISHMENT OF SCHOOL DEVELOPMENT PLAN

BUDGETARY PROCESS

to address in your plans, and will help determine the form the plans will take.

It is both unfair and irresponsible for governors to have to be involved in defining and planning their expectations for the school and then to have to wait a whole year to see how things are going. Of course, there is a balance to be struck. No one wants or needs governors to interfere every five minutes, but you should expect regular reporting.

One of the most important questions that inspectors ask governors is "How did you know what to do and what was going on?" Special measures* too often come as a surprise to governing bodies that either just did not know what was going on or, less often, that have been deceived.

The head's report to governors is the main mechanism through which you get an update on the aspects of school life and work that have been identified in the SDP. The head-teacher should share a frank assessment of how the pupils and staff are progressing and what the emerging issues and problems are. This can be backed up with school visits that enable governors to see if their plans and policies are appropriate and to get staff feedback. Parent and pupil surveys may provide useful information – it is worth noting that inspections are to start canvassing pupil views.

External help is often available. From time to time the head and governors may ask for a second opinion from an external adviser or consultant. This person may often be the School Improvement Partner* (SIP), one of whose jobs is to advise the governors in conducting the head's review. (SIPs will not be in place in all primary schools until April 2008.)

Governors should properly concern themselves with pupil and staff morale, the site and buildings, the provision of the curriculum, the relationship with parents and the wider community, and the leadership and organisation of the school. Monitoring by governors of progress on all these fronts is essential.

Evaluating the The governing body shares in the accountability for how the
outcomes school is doing and is required to give account, not least to
parents. One way of assessing the school's progress is
through the two or three governors appointed by the governing body to conduct the headteacher's annual performance review. The governing body also reviews the performance of pupils in public examinations and tests. But these
are not be the only measures and indicators available to you.

There is a framework which you can follow so as to be
able to make a sensible judgement on the school's progress
and consider what further actions need to be taken. The
framework has five points:

1. How well are we doing?
Look at percentages and charts that show you how the
school is progressing against its previous and current attainment targets. These may be provided by the school, the LA
or the DCSF.

2. How well should we be doing?
Identify targets that make sense in terms of the school's situation and values. They should take account of national and
local benchmarks where relevant, even if these seem challenging and are getting more complex. The data upon which
to base this will include evidence of performance to date,
comprising the results of any internal school assessment
regimes, LA-provided benchmarking data and RAISEonline
from the DCSF.

3. What more should we aim to achieve this year?
In the light of all the circumstances, the resources, the nature
of the intake, our previous performance and that of similar
schools, what can realistically be achieved?

4. What must we do to make it happen?
There should be a flexible plan for managing change, with a
focus on teaching and learning.

5. How can we make sure it does happen?

There should be clear responsibilities for monitoring the work of the plan, using outside support and examining reports and results in the light of the targets and objectives that have been agreed. Individual governors or the appropriate committee may monitor different aspects of the plan and report back to the governing body.

There are other indicators and outcomes at our disposal for judging the school's performance, such as:

- the number of potential new parents putting the school as a first or second preference

- the number of pupils who leave the school other than at the statutory time, and the reasons for leaving

- the pupil attendance rates

- the number of exclusions

- staff turnover rate

- staff promotions

- teacher absences through sickness

- the cost of furniture and repairs

- the level of community and government investment in the school, such as School Achievement Awards.

The figures need to be handled with care as they often do not correlate to performance in a simple way, but they do provided evidence that needs assessment.

Making judgements

"Too often in education it is argued that our achievements cannot be assessed because our situation is unique. Uniqueness is more often claimed to excuse apparently poor performance than to explain good."
K. Aspinwall *et al. Managing Evaluation in Education: a development approach*, Routlege, 1992

No set of data or information is on its own going to provide a definitive guide to a school's performance. However, when one does suggest that something is amiss, it is too easy to shrug it off as exceptional, unfair or irrelevant. We should be wary of such excuses. If an attempt is made to sweep aside evidence of a weakness, then we need to call for further evidence, or query the grounds for claiming irrelevance and satisfy ourselves that they are valid.

Governors themselves sometimes query their right as voluntary lay people to pass an opinion or judgement on their school. This is unnecessarily self-effacing. Parents and the community at large show no hesitation in jumping to a conclusion about what a school is like, more often than not on slender evidence. The pupils are well aware of what the school is or is not doing for them. All of these judgements can have far more serious consequences than most of the judgements that the governors make. Parents can remove their children!

It is precisely because most governors are not professionally involved in education that they are valuable. Understanding the reasons for a school's success may require special expertise, but the fact of that success should be clear to the ordinary observer, if it is genuine.

The governors are there to get to know the school on behalf of the community. When you need professional input you should not let natural reticence lead you to forgetting that you have professionals among you all the time in the persons of the head and staff governors, and you should trust their contribution unless you have reason not to.

But heads and teachers alike recognise the danger of myopia that comes from living close to the action day in, day out. In essence, and at its best, the governing body is a space where new perspectives are offered, vital connections are made and the vision of the improving school is sustained. In the words of Tony Wright MP: "What is new is the combination of lay and professional insight, each incapable on its own but capable of fusing a dynamic partnership that is greater than its parts and with real potential."

Getting down to business 4

Once you have grasped the model, putting joined-up governance into practice need not be difficult. Effective governance requires efficient organisation of the business, which means keeping focused on the key tasks and priorities and not getting deflected by unnecessary detail. The governing body is most effective when it makes sure things are being done that should be done – not trying to do them themselves.

This is not to say that things will always go smoothly. Keeping to the agenda, having fairly but firmly chaired meetings and always having just the right information supplied when you need it will be easier said than done on many occasions. But if the business is run smoothly you will be surprised how much time and energy is released for concentrating on the key strategic discussions and decisions. Ensuring that you make the best use of meetings and work effectively as a team is the key.

Hopefully, the days are now gone when governing body meetings commonly drifted on into the late evening, when no-one had the energy or inclination to make important decisions. Indeed, the best governing bodies will probably find their meetings last no longer than two hours. This should not be taken as a signal to play down the importance of the formal meeting – far from it. The formal termly meeting – or half-termly, which is now more usual – is critical because of the authority vested in the meeting. But the meeting must be focused.

The governing body meeting

The chair The role of the chair of the meeting is, of course, vital. Good chairs are worth their weight in gold. It is a time-consuming and onerous job, because it extends far beyond the time spent in meetings. The DCSF now communicates directly with chairs on most issues, and there is a lot of information to digest. So chairs need to be able to give the time to the paperwork, absorb what they need to know for their own governing body, and then direct and "sift" everything that could be governing body business. But the most important aspect of the role of the chair is in leadership. Much has been written about the role of the head as the leading professional in a school, but the chair also needs to be a good leader, and should partner the head in leadership.

For the chair of a governing body leadership means having a clear vision of the role of the governing body and how that is to be exercised. A good chair will set the tone for the way in which the business is conducted – especially in the full meetings. The following checklist for chairs recommends four rules for chairs to keep meetings effective and efficient.

Checklist for chairs

- *Keep the agenda relevant, manageable and not too long.*

- *Keep the meeting "on track": discussions should be focused; no-one should speak too much or for too long; and the agenda should be completed in good time.*

- *Set a tone for the meeting which is "inclusive": make sure everyone has a chance to speak; do not tolerate language or behaviour that is sexist, racist or in any other way prejudiced; keep discussions jargon-free; and introduce new governors or observers such as school staff.*

- *Ensure the minutes of the meeting are clear and concise but adequately reflect the meeting, with actions noted against the responsible person; work with the clerk in the meeting to achieve this.*

The agenda

The governing body in each school sets its own agenda for each meeting. Some LAs produce a draft agenda for governing bodies; this can be a good starting point, but it is for the chair of each governing body, with the headteacher and the clerk, to formulate the appropriate agenda and not to feel that it is being imposed by anyone else. The agenda is a working tool and when the chair, head and clerk draw it up they are in fact leading the governing body in what needs to be done. However, it should also be an open process so any governor can have the opportunity to put items forward.

→ page 49

Some governing bodies find a timed agenda* helpful in avoiding overlong meetings – on the basis that the most important items get the most appropriate time and more formal items get the minimum. Timed agendas should not, however, be used inflexibly as this can constrain debate.

Asterisked terms are defined in the Glossary, pages 116-21

Anything other than the briefest Any Other Business is not recommended as good practice since it runs the risk of new discussions with which not all governors will be familiar. If you must have it, it should only be used for urgent matters, and these should be raised with the chair before the meeting begins so that they can consider what action to recommend. A good chair will note the items raised and then give them sufficient preparation and air time at a subsequent meeting of the full governing body, committee or working group, if necessary seeking approval for chair's action.

The agenda for most governing bodies will have many standard items, together with a major issue from the annual cycle of key responsibilities, such as approving the budget or the annual report. It is advisable to give this a prominent position early on in the business. A list of the standard items is given on the next page.

Some governing bodies like to print a note at the head of the agenda which reminds all governors of the importance of the equal opportunity to make contributions. The statement might read: "This governing body respects the different voices of all governors regardless of gender, ethnicity, age

Suggested standard items for the agenda

• *Apologies – consent to absence is extremely important since regulations automatically disqualify governors for non-attendance over six months*

• *Minutes of the last meeting*

• *Matters arising*

• *Minutes of committee meetings and working parties – it is essential that all committees with delegated authority should report back in writing to the full governing body as soon as possible*

• *Declaration of interests – any governor with a conflict of interest in any item should declare it and the governing body can then decide if they need to withdraw from the proceedings*

• *Register of Business Interests – should be keep up to date when there are new governors and should be reviewed annually.*

• *Report back on chair's action*

• *Headteacher's report*

• *Governor training – many governing bodies have a link governor; this is their chance to review and reflect on current needs*

• *Any ad hoc issues*

or ability, believes in creating equal opportunities at all times for all governors to make a full and effective contribution to the governance of the school, and will ensure that appropriate support is given to achieve this whenever possible."

If there are any confidential items for discussion these should be signalled by the chair at the start of the meeting, and minuted on a separate sheet. It is useful to print the confidential minutes on a differently coloured paper from the main minutes so that they are easily identified.

The clerk Each governing body has to have a clerk – who cannot be one of its members. Many LAs offer a clerking service, which is usually good value. Alternatively, governing bodies employ their own clerk, or agree that the job is one of the responsibilities of a school bursar or administrator.

It is increasingly being acknowledged that an efficient clerk is an essential support to the governing body. It is therefore essential to ensure that your clerk is trained and kept up to date with new regulations and guidance – again this service may be offered by the LA. The ISCG handbook, *A Manual for Governing Bodies and their Clerks*, is a very useful source of information on the clerk's functions. A good clerk is indispensable to the chair in ensuring that governing body business is conducted in accordance with regulations, as well as sharing the workload with correspondence and minutes. The clerk should also be trained and available to clerk the statutory committees of the governing body – other → pages 86–7 governing body committees may be clerked by a member of the committee.

Working with the headteacher in meetings

A good working relationship between the governing body and headteacher is essential to successful governance. As the leading professional, the headteacher should regard his or her work with the governing body as an integral part of managing the school. The governing body in turn should only make reasonable demands on the headteacher. These will mainly be for information and for reports that it would expect to be supplied as good management practice; for example, you would need information from the headteacher on pupil performance to discuss and decide on pupil achievement targets.

The headteacher is automatically an *ex officio* governor unless they choose not to be. Most are. Those who are not are still expected to attend governing body meetings and present reports; the main difference from those who are governors is that they will have no vote in governing body decisions.

The regular headteacher's report* is an essential tool in

the exercise of your monitoring and review role. If you have two full governing body meetings a term, it is not usually necessary to take a report at every meeting, but there should be at least one each term. The report should be presented in written form and sent out with the agenda so that everyone can study it in advance and prepare any questions. This will save time in the meeting. A diary of events and a list of visitors is *not* what is required, and it is a good idea if the governing body, probably through the chair, agrees with the head in advance what sort of information it might require during the year. This should fit in with the monitoring and review cycle. The headteacher should therefore expect questions and discussion on the information presented in the report and be able to reflect on proposals made and decisions sought. In many cases discussion on the report will be at the heart of the meeting – it is not a case of raising questions only when something is amiss.

Formal or informal? Governing body meetings must, of course, follow a formal pattern, and decisions must be clearly agreed and recorded. Although most governing bodies have very reasonably moved away from a formal structure of resolutions with proposers and seconders, it is important that policies and procedures are still formally agreed, and that when a vote has to be taken the numbers are recorded.

Beyond this, a certain amount of informality can be "good for business" since it encourages all governors to contribute in a relaxed manner. New governors in particular often find formal meetings intimidating, and any opportunity should be taken to address this. But if the chair is summing up the view of the meeting on an issue without having taken a formal vote, they should make this clear in case any governor wishes to object or seek clarification. Summing up a discussion in this way would normally also be clearly reflected in the way the minutes are phrased.

If you usually get through the business in an efficient way, you may feel there is time to schedule time at the beginning or during the meeting for tea or coffee. These social moments are valuable as they give governors who otherwise only see each other in formal meetings the opportunity to get to know each other – and the headteacher – better.

Much of the full meeting may be a matter of report because of the delegated authority to committees, groups and individuals, such as the chair. This function should in no way be dismissed as unimportant. You should make sure that you do read and understand committee reports and other information supplied, and that you are happy that sub-groups are working clearly within their delegated powers. The inclusive governing body will encourage committee chairs or other members of the committee to speak briefly to their reports. This enables different "voices" to be heard.

Reporting back

Questions to a committee chair on why decisions were taken in a particular way might be appropriate, but reports should not be discussed again in the full meeting unless there is an irregularity – for example, where there appears to have been a breach of policy or delegated authority. If any governor believes any individual, committee or group has acted *ultra vires* (outside the authority delegated to them) they should be given the opportunity to raise and discuss this. The same applies to any other report back.

However, some matters may have been reported back by a committee for a formal decision or ratification by the full governing body. These will require full discussion. A good example of this is the annual budget; it can be approved by a committee, but most governing bodies delegate the drafting to a finance committee while reserving approval for the whole governing body. The finance committee will draw up the draft budget, possibly over several meetings, and will then be required to lead a discussion at the full governing body. For a governing body simply to take their recommendations without explanation would not be appropriate.

Working as a team It is already clear from the number of contributions to meetings that governing bodies do not function efficiently without working as a team. All members of the governing body as well as the chair, the headteacher and the clerk, should be encouraged to play their part. The chair should see encouraging team-working as part of the leadership role, although this can sometimes stretch their powers of persuasion with those governors who are used to taking a back seat. The time invested will be well spent if it results in all governors making a contribution.

The strength of any governing body lies in the wealth of experience and expertise and the different perspectives around the table. Everyone does have something to offer, although some people may have more limited time to get involved than others, and it is important that jobs are shared. It is particularly important that the chair is supported and does not accrue too many roles. For example, committee chairs' and clerks' functions could be shared so that no one person is holding more than one office. Even though the chair of governors may attend most of the committee meetings they are there only as one among equals.

Many governing bodies find that their sense of working as a team is enhanced by having whole-governing-body training. Most LAs will offer such courses, where a trainer comes out and spends an evening with the governing body. You may even choose teamwork as the subject of the course, although it will still be very valuable for team-building if the subject is itself some other aspect of governing body work.

An annual timetable Getting through the business is most effective if it is planned well ahead so that governors and staff know at what point in the year executive decisions about staffing and finance have to be made. This makes the planning of meetings easier and will indicate when more frequent meetings of certain committees might be required. The most obvious example of this is the work of the finance committee in budget setting, which usually takes place over a few weeks in the spring term between receiving the LA budgets and reconciling the school budget.

The cyclical nature of the joined-up model also indicates points in the school year when monitoring and review should take place and new plans be drawn up and implemented. So, for example, setting pupil achievement targets and the review of the headteacher's performance must take place in the autumn term. There should therefore be monitoring mechanisms in place during the spring and summer terms, which should fit in with the School Development Plan cycle.

Some schools are now having an annual review day when staff and governors together examine the SDP and plan for the year ahead. While this is yet another commitment for governors, if best use is made of the time it should provide the blueprint for governing body business throughout the following year, and will save time later – not to mention the important opportunity such a day affords for governors and staff to work together and build a constructive partnership.

A suggested annual timetable for the work of the governing body is given overleaf.

Working in committees and working groups

Doing much of the work of the governing body in committee has been shown to be a very effective way of working. Not only does it relieve the pressure of business in the main meetings, but it also provides a more appropriate environment for discussion and deliberation about the details of policy. It also spreads the workload and makes for teamwork, as many governors find they can make a much more worthwhile contribution to the work of the governing body in committee than in the necessarily more formal full governors' meeting. Committee work is particularly useful for policy development work, including monitoring and evaluating policies in practice.

Annual cycle of governing body work

AUTUMN TERM

Statutory	Optional
chair and vice chair – elect (though they can be elected for up to four years)	*operating guidelines for the gb - discuss*
committees and working parties – appoint	*objectives of the gb for the year - set*
terms of reference of committees – review	*programme of meetings for the year, including committees – agree*
admissions policy for the next school year – consult other admission authorities (schools that are admission authorities only)	*review of previous year's work and identification of future work*
	SATs/public examination results/national tests – review
	destinations of leavers – review
	link governor – appoint
	individual governors' curriculum responsibilities – review
	school development targets – set
	SDP – review

SPRING TERM

Statutory	Optional
pay policy – review	*curriculum plans for the coming year – agree*
budget – agree	*staffing structure – agree*
school prospectus (if this was not done in the autumn term) – agree new edition	*future work – identify*
admissions arrangements for following autumn – publish proposals (schools that are admission authorities only)	*SDP – review progress*

SUMMER TERM

Statutory	Optional
salaries – provide the head, deputy and all teachers with details of the statement of their position on the salary spine effective from 1 September	evaluate governing body's effectiveness over the past year, relating this to targets set in the autumn term
Performance Management Policy – review	attendance of pupils and staff – review
	pupil exclusions for the year – review
	future work – identify
	SDP – review progress

ON A REGULAR BASIS

Optional

monitor School Development Plan

write new policies/review existing policies

support and training for governors

governors' visits to the school

reports from the Students' Council

report by governor/committee with responsibility for SEN

report by individual governors on their curriculum areas

AT ANY TIME IN YEAR

Statutory	Optional
School Profile (England) or Annual Report to Parents (Wales) – publication	induction of new governors
	inspection – preparation
Annual Meeting for Parents (Wales)	monitor Workforce Agreement reforms
clerk – appoint	Friends Association/PTA/PSA – report
revise the SEF (can be more than once a year if necessary)	

Accountability

→ pages 26–8

→ page 92

Most of the governing body's work can be delegated to committees but committees can only work within the authority the governing body gives them, as discussed in chapter 1. Carefully drawing up the remit for each committee is therefore crucial. This is also why it is essential that committees report back on their work to the main governing body. In some cases, there cannot be any more than the most general discussion in the full governing body. For example, if a staff appeals panel had heard a case where a member of staff thought they has been unjustly refused promotion "across the threshold" it would be inappropriate to identify the individual or give enough information to let them be identified.

→ page 23

A full list of the responsibilities that can be delegated appears in the DCSF Decision Planner, referred to earlier. The guidance indicates what decisions can be delegated to the head, what have to be made by the governing body and what have to be made by the head.

Appeals and complaints

Some specific responsibilities of the governing body either have to be or should be delegated to committees or panels. These are:

- Exclusions
  A committee must meet in accordance with statutory guidance to review pupil exclusions. The committee should comprise either three or five governors with a quorum of three. Neither the head nor a non-governor can be a member.

- Staff Appeals
  The committee meets to hear an appeal against dismissal by a member of staff, or to hear a complaint by a member of staff about their pay or position. Each committee should comprise three or more governors. The headteacher cannot be a member of the committee.

- Appointing a new head or deputy
  Although the actual decision on who to appoint has to be

taken by the whole governing body, the selection and interview procedure should be conducted by a specially established panel.

The governing body does not have to appoint members to the first two panels at the beginning of the year, but might agree a pool of people who will be drawn on as and when necessary. The selection committee is normally formed only when needed.

Governors also have to be appointed to carry out the head's performance management review, but they do not constitute a committee. This is discussed later in this chapter. → page 92

Most governing bodies find the following committees, or combination of committees, helpful in their work:

- Finance
  This deals with the financial responsibilities for the delegated budget, including drafting the budget for the governing body to approve, and monitoring the budget during the year.

- Premises (often combined with Finance)
  This meets to carry out responsibilities for the school premises and grounds.

- Personnel, Staffing or Pay
  This meets to deal with personnel issues, including the recruitment of staff. It can make sense for the committee members also to constitute the group of governors with delegated authority to review the performance of the headteacher.

- Pastoral or Discipline
  This handles responsibilities for behaviour and discipline within school, including pupil attendance.

- Curriculum Committee (sometimes called the School Development Plan Committee since this can be the prime focus of the group)

This carries out the governors' responsibilities for the national curriculum and assessment, including sex education and religious education. It may include special educational needs.

- Health and Safety
  This carries out responsibilities for health and safety for pupils and staff including school security. Some of these responsibilities may be covered by the remits of other committees, for example the Premises Committee may consider school security. Pupil safety may be considered by the Pastoral Committee, and the health and safety of staff may be considered by the Personnel Committee.

- Special Educational Needs
  Although this area can be included in a Pastoral Committee or in a Curriculum Committee, some governing bodies like to have a separate group working on SEN. At the very minimum, each governing body should have a "responsible person" for SEN, who may be a governor or the head. This has developed into a very successful role, and the majority of SEN governors make a very supportive and constructive contribution in partnership with the school's SEN co-ordinator (usually known as the SENCO).

Although the LA is responsible for assessing children with special educational needs, the governing body also has statutory responsibilities to ensure that the school has a policy in line with the national Code of Practice, and that the policy is fairly and adequately applied for all children with SEN. (For further information see the *Guide to the Law*, chapter 8.) Most LAs provide specific training for SEN governors.

The purpose of a committee system must

Committees – possible structure

Finance & General Purposes (budget monitoring, premises, health & safety, security)

Curriculum / School Development Planning (target-setting, RE & collective worship, SEN, sex education)

Personnel/Pay (staffing, pay policy, annual salary review)

Pastoral (discipline policy, behaviour, pupil attendance, SEN) always be to facilitate effective governance. This means not making work for committees, nor committees making work for the governing body! So if there is no need for a committee, don't have one! If responsibilities can usefully be combined – such as finance and premises – then do so. Use *ad hoc* working parties if they are more appropriate to the task, and dissolve them when the work is done (see below).

There is, in fact, no compulsion on any governing body to have any committees other than the exclusion and staff dismissal/grievance panels, and, especially if yours is a small school, you may elect to have no committees and do all the work in the full governing body.

Working groups

When you have a topic that needs particular attention but which is not going to be part of regular governing body business, it can be appropriate to set up a working group or working party, as we saw in chapter 1. The constitution, working practices and remit of a working group are entirely up to the governing body to decide, but a working group cannot make any decisions for the governing body, nor act on its behalf. When appropriate a working group reports its findings or recommendations to the full governing body, which then makes whatever decisions it considers appropriate.

→ pages 26–7

Examples of when you might feel it necessary to set up a working group would include doing a study of changing to trust status, or exploring parents' views of the extended services the school should provide.

A working group can provide a good opportunity to involve non-governors.

Terms of reference

The full governing body is responsible for determining the subject to be covered and way of working of each committee. These are stated in the committee's terms of reference, which have to be reviewed annually for all committees. The terms of reference should include the membership, the remit, the quorum and the procedures for conducting the business,

Annual cycle of committee work

Items in roman type *have to be considered each year, by the full governing body if there is no designated committee. See also pages 84–6, remembering that many of the items there can also be delegated to committees.*

AUTUMN TERM

Curriculum and Special Needs

Elect Chair

Agree clerking arrangements

School Development Policy planning

Policy review

Review SEN policy

Appoint SEN governor (if appropriate)

Set targets for KS2, 3 and 4 (England)

Finance and Building

Elect Chair

Agree clerking arrangements

School Development Plan

Monitor budget

Appoint governor(s) for Health & Safety

Review staff salary points

Personnel

Elect Chair

Agree clerking arrangements

School Development Plan

Appoint governors to conduct head's performance management review

Review and determine the head's salary (*backdated to 1 September*)

SUMMER TERM

Curriculum and Special Needs

Review and monitor specified curriculum area

Review pupil exclusions for the year

Review pupil attendance

Finance and Building

Present budget for next year to full governing body (if not done in Spring)

Audit school fund

Staff salaries review

Personnel

Review job descriptions

Review pupil and staff attendance

Review Performance Management policy

Review staff salaries and provide details to staff

SPRING TERM

Curriculum and Special Needs

Report on curriculum developments

Finalise any curriculum plans for the coming year

SEN report

Finance and Building

Draft budget for next year

Review letting policy

Review insurance

School Development Plan

Review whole-school pay policy

Personnel

Review staff structure

Review whole-school pay policy

which generally need to accord with those of the full governing body.

The procedures should ensure adequate notice is given of meetings, including sending out an agenda and relevant reports in due time, that a chair (who cannot be anyone employed in the school) and a minutes secretary or clerk (who, except for exclusions and appeals panels, can be a governor or a member of staff) are correctly appointed, and that clear minutes are produced for all governors at the next full meeting. Committees can include associate governors, and can give them voting rights; this can be a useful way of including relevant school staff or others with appropriate expertise, perhaps on an *ad hoc* basis.

Working with others

Governors are volunteers. You should not be expected to be an expert in anything. If you are, then this is a bonus for which the school will be grateful.

All the same, many governors have become anxious about some of the responsibilities they have been asked to take on, particularly reviewing the performance of the headteacher, as they do not feel they have the necessary expertise. This is an understandable concern. It is one of the reasons why an independent adviser was initially made available to work with governors on the head's performance review; this task falls to School Improvement Partners as they come into place.

The annual review of the headteacher's performance must be carried out by two or three governors (governors who are members of staff are excluded). When the system was set up an independent adviser was made available for the task. The governors got eight hours of their time free of charge, which was intended for them to give advice and attend the review meetings.

When the government determined the role of School Improvement Partners*(SIPs) it decided that they should take over this function. SIPs started in secondary schools in

September 2006, but the phase-in into primary schools was planned over a longer period, up to April 2008. Until that time primary schools without SIPs continue to receive the help of an independent adviser.

Although the SIP is otherwise employed to challenge and support the headteacher, governors could ask them for advice on other matters outside of the head's performance review. Their main concern is school improvement, and they will look hard at how the school is performing and bring an external perspective to bear. They should therefore have a knowledge of the school that can help governors in making their own judgements and decisions.

There are many other possibilities for profiting from the expertise of professional advisers.

Financial advisers are often available to help draw up the school's budget, and, for maintained schools that do not have their own bank account, can advise on the monthly financial statements sent to the school. LA officers, particularly those responsible for governor support and training, are another valuable source of help and advice. In forging a constructive partnership with schools both officers and advisers will attend full meetings, committees or training events with governors if invited with reasonable notice. Make the best use of their expertise and experience.

Working with advisers is becoming more common, particularly in areas where governing bodies feel they are lacking in experience. You could bring in professional advisers for particular issues, such as budget-setting and monitoring, or as associate members of a committee or working group. Governors involved in contracting out any school services or entering into a private finance initiatives can find themselves hiring legal advice or architects, although this is expensive.

But always remember that external advisers are just that – sources of advice. They are working for you, the governing body, and it is still you – as agents of local community accountability – who decide on policy and make the final decisions.

This applies equally to the SIP's role in the headteacher's performance review, although, of course, you should give serious consideration to their advice.

Other schools Schools are increasingly encouraged by government to collaborate with each other, and there are a number of instances where a group of up to six schools has federated, with a single governing body and headteacher for all the schools.

Without necessarily going this far schools can benefit from sharing expertise. Headteachers have been doing this for some time, with local schools forming clusters whose headteachers have regular meetings with each other. Governors have rarely been involved with these, but the provision of extended services means that they will need increasingly to work with governors in other schools. Many of the services that a school is expected to provide – even something as apparently straightforward as a breakfast club – will not be viable for small schools on their own. But working with other neighbouring schools can produce a cost benefit and avoid duplication of effort.

Moreover, governing bodies are required to establish what a community needs before providing extended services. Your definition of "community" might be too limited if it is restricted to the immediate neighbourhood of your school without taking in those of nearby schools.

There is a lot more to collaboration that this. For example, delivery of the 14-19 curriculum means secondary schools offering work experience and courses that they may not be able to provide themselves. While the former will mean working with local employers, the latter is likely to mean collaboration with other schools or further education colleges. Forms of collaboration between schools are many and growing; increasingly governing bodies need to consider their schools operating outside their physical boundaries when they are deciding on their strategic plans.

An effective governing body needs to reflect on how well it is doing and identify where support is needed. Good governing bodies don't just happen – they are formed and shaped to work well together as a team. This usually means getting a balance between youth and experience, as well as ensuring the body is as representative as it can be. Above all, a good governing body comprises governors who bring sufficient energy and enthusiasm to make sure they do a good job. As a volunteer group, this certainly means making sure all governors, both as individuals and as a team, get the support and training they need in order to make an effective contribution. As a minimum this means induction for new governors, refresher sessions for more experienced governors (particularly on new government initiatives or changes in the law), training for chairs and members of appeals panels, and training for those who clerk committees. All governors also need access to information and guidance to help them in their day-to-day work as governors.

How well are you doing?

Training and support

Training, information and support come from three main sources and in a variety of forms.

The main source should be your LA. LAs have a statutory duty to provide training and support for all governors, and extra support for governors of schools causing concern. Most LAs have a governor training co-ordinator or other officer with this responsibility, who can provide you with a programme of training. Mostly this is offered as a package for schools to buy annually, with training sessions then being free to individual governors.

Training sessions are usually offered on particular topics, and take place in the evening or at weekends. Customised sessions can generally be requested by individual governing bodies on issues that concern them – or are sometimes organised for a group of schools. Many LAs also offer useful topic packs and updates on the law. LAs will have a direct governor telephone line and most have a dedicated web-page on their council's website.

Secondly, the DCSF has developed training packs, including one on performance management and a course for chairs and potential chairs. Your LA will offer courses based on them, and there are on-line versions but these are recommended only if you cannot attend the course. DCSF guidance documents are also available free of charge and are usually posted on the DCSF website, which is a useful source of information that is worth frequent visits.

The third source is public bodies and private companies. Organisations such as Ofsted and the Audit Commission produce helpful publications for governors from time to time. The National Governors' Association (NGA) produces

→ page 122 publications for governors, notably the very comprehensive Papers on individual issues, and a regular magazine. There are some good publications from commercial publishers too – the publisher of this book offers a range. For particular queries there is also a national governor helpline where the advice is free (Governorline – 08000 722 181).

Training for governors is usually very good value for money, and each governing body should encourage governors to keep up to date and develop appropriate skills. Many LAs encourage each governing body to have a link governor to liaise with their training unit.

Self-review An effective governing body will feel effective. It's a bit like getting physically fit – you just start to feel better and find it is easier to sprint when required. Many governing bodies now carry out a "healthcheck" on themselves every year or so to see how they are progressing towards this goal. This can be an important opportunity to reflect critically on how you do things and where you could improve. It is certainly a good idea in preparation for an Ofsted inspection.

Many local authorities have developed a self-evaluation framework for governing bodies, often as part of school self-review, which they will offer you if asked. Often they will start you on it in a whole-governing-body training session.

Public accountability   5

"Accountability is seen as a requirement to have one's work tested, debated and judged within some more or less formal structure. Success may not be rewarded or failure punished, but there is an obligation to give reasons for action, to review outcomes and to submit to judgement on the performance, in all the circumstances, of the task which one accepts is one's own."

> Joan Sallis, *Schools, Parents and Governors: A new approach to accountability*, Routledge, 1988

In chapter 1 the importance of the public accountability of the governing body was highlighted. Schools within the state system are a public service, funded by public funds. Whoever manages and governs our schools should therefore be accountable to the public.

When LAs and the central state had responsibility for running schools, they were accountable through the ballot box, centrally and locally. Now that headteachers and governing bodies have much of that responsibility, accountability has to function through other channels. The system we work with provides direct accountability to the public, as headteachers and managers are accountable in their school to the governing body, which is representative of the different public groups that have an interest in the school. In turn, the governing body, like any representative body, is accountable to the people it represents, in this case the public.

This does not mean that the ballot box is not still relevant, as the local authority is run by local elected members who are accountable for its statutory duties, and central government, whose policy directs the state system, is chosen by the public every four or five years through general elections.

As now enshrined in regulations, governors may have a prime responsibility to raise educational standards, but as "trustees of public funds" and "guardians of the curriculum" our prime purpose is to exercise accountability on behalf of the public in the state system of education. As explained in chapter 1, this purpose is best met by our acting as "critical friends" of the school. This means giving support but at the same time always seeking to improve by challenging current practice, assumptions, expectations, plans and priorities.

→ pages 21–3

However, although "critical friendship" is at the heart of the relationship between the headteacher and the governing body, this way of approaching accountability can risk creating an adversarial relationship. The inclusion of the headteacher in the membership of the governing body – and few choose not to be governors – should help avoid this. All the same, the danger remains, and a lot rests on the manner in which questions and points to the head are expressed. Challenging does not mean being aggressive, and challenges that are seen as valid and well-made should help build respect.

The deliberations of the full governing body should include a self-reflective element on how current priorities can be challenged in the interests of continuous improvement. If you have the regular self-review as outlined in the previous chapter, it should ensure that you operate in this way.

→ page 96

Public accountability is a two-way dialogue. As elected or appointed representatives of the local stakeholders in the school – parents, staff, the LA, the local community and perhaps the Church, other foundation bodies or trusts – the prime responsibility of the governing body is to ensure a well-run school and steer it in the direction of future

→ pages 8–9

improvement. That this body is comprised of all the appropriate "public" voices and interests is the way in which the state ensures that the public service is directed by the public it serves. It follows, therefore, that the public who are being represented should be kept informed of how the governing body itself is performing. The governing body, with significant statutory responsibilities, must therefore be corporately accountable to all the stakeholders it represents. This can best be described as corporate accountability in four directions – all of which highlight the central relationship between schools and the public: accountability to parents; accountability to the state at locally elected level through the LA; accountability to the state at centrally elected level through Ofsted; and accountability to the general public.

Accountability to parents

Parents – surely it goes without saying? – should be the prime constituency to which schools and governing bodies are accountable. The question for us all is how best to achieve this. In one sense schools are accountable to parents because they sit "*in loco parentis*" for their children. But beyond this, the parent-school landscape has changed remarkably in recent years, and there are now much higher expectations of regular communication and information from both sides. Parents want to have detailed and up-to-date knowledge of how their children are progressing at school, while schools want parents to be involved and supportive. The value of this has been shown where schools make formal arrangements to ensure that parents are involved in their children's education, as they have been able to demonstrate more effective learning and progress. Some secondary schools now have a parents' forum to discuss policy issues and some primary schools invite parents into the classroom to support the child with reading or other tasks on a regular basis.

Home School Agreement

Asterisked terms are defined in the Glossary, pages 116–21

Since September 1999 it has been a requirement for all schools to have a Home–School Agreement* where the school and parents set out their expectations of and commitments to each other. Its aim is to formally secure a constructive relationship in the best interests of the pupils.

The law states that the agreement should be reviewed "from time to time", but does not indicate the timescale any more accurately than this. This could well be an annual or biennial job for a governors' communications committee. The initial construction of this document will have been a prime concern of the governing body, and its review is also an important job. As with drafting the initial agreement, review is practically useless if parents are not consulted and the agreement is just foisted on them by the school. Parent governors are the appropriate people to carry out this consultation.

Home-School Agreements tend to focus on how both the school and the parents will support individual pupils. It is therefore only in part a mechanism for accountability to parents, much more an expression of mutual expectation.

Reporting to parents

Until recently, governing bodies in England and Wales were obliged to account formally to parents on an annual basis through the linked Annual Governors' Report to Parents* and the Annual Parents' Meeting*. In 2005 these were abolished in England, and, even though they remain in Wales, governing bodies there can avoid holding the annual meeting if they announce their intention not to have one and fewer than 15 parents object.

The demise of the annual meeting was probably inevitable as the meetings were generally very sparsely attended. However, even if normally there were no issues that drew parents in, the existence of the meeting meant that there was a forum for those occasions when it was really needed. It is now up to governing bodies to provide whatever mechanism they consider best suited to their school for parents to question them about their work and to be consulted on their views.

In some cases schools have done this by continuing to hold an annual meeting – just because it is not compulsory to have one it does not mean that you can't have one. More commonly schools hold meetings for parents when there are specific issues to discuss. The Self-Evaluation Form provided by Ofsted requires schools to ask parents how satisfied they are with the school and includes a questionnaire that can be used to do this. Although the document is short, it can indicate areas of concern that need further discussion between governors and parents. Another method that is used by some governing bodies to discharge their accountability to parents is for a number of governors to attend parents' evenings, perhaps with their own table, so that parents can come and talk to them. Or you could establish a rule whereby if a certain number of parents demanded a meeting for all parents the governing body would hold one.

Under the Education and Inspections Act of 2006 trust schools are required to set up parent councils if their governing body is constituted so that most of the parent governors are appointed by the trust rather than being elected. This has been designed to provide parents with a voice in such schools. The Act also encourages other schools to set up parent councils, even though it is not a statutory requirement. An active and representative parent council can provide a governing body with a means of accounting for itself to parents, and can also enable parent governors to better consult with parents to discover their views.

For governors in Wales, who have to produce an annual report, the report is meant to be a team effort between governors and staff – and you might also usefully include the pupils – not a job to be got out of the way by a couple of noble volunteers. If it is done this way, with a clear idea of what is to go into it, and the writing shared among a large number of people, producing the report can be an extremely worthwhile exercise in building positive relationships. If you can use the report to engage parents in a discussion about the future as well as accounting for the past, it can set up the meeting as a useful consultative mechanism.

Instead of an annual report, English governors are required to complete a School Profile each year. This is an electronic, on-line document, and once it has been done the governing body should notify parents of its availability and where they can access it. For those parents who do not have internet access hard copies should be made available at school.

The School Profile consists of several sections where governors give information about the school in answer to certain questions. Each school downloads its own template, which is only available once the DCSF has completed the section that summarises the school's results in public exams and National Curriculum tests. As the content is prescribed, the Profile does not allow for information on all matters that you may wish parents to know about, such as how the budget has been spent or the work of the governing body itself. Moreover, the fact that parents have to make some effort to access the Profile means that it might be less read than a document which arrives on their kitchen tables.

It is therefore advisable to look at additional ways of being accountable to parents, such as a regular newsletter or some of the means suggested above. The governing body needs to bear in mind that it has a serious responsibility to account to parents for the exercise of its duties. For as long as governing bodies have significant responsibility for the direction of the school, adequate and accurate reporting to parents will be important in protecting the integrity of good governance, even if no formal methods are prescribed by government.

Accountability to the LA The governing body is also accountable to its local authority (LA). All schools within the state system are "maintained"* by their LAs, and the governing body has statutory responsibility for the school which is legally delegated from the Secretary of State to the LA, and from the LA to the governing body. Since the governing body only has authority by virtue of this delegation from the LA it is surprising that LAs have not required greater accountability from governing bodies. While it has always been a right of the LA to hold the governing body to account by requesting appropriate information, in practice this has not really been exercised. The ultimate accountability sanction, that the LA withdraw delegation of the budget to the governing body, has always existed but is rarely used.

The *Code of Practice on LEA-School Relations* that came into force in 1999 (at a time when local education authorities – LEAs – still existed), however, re-emphasised the importance of a constructive relationship and the powers of intervention of the LA in the interests of school improvement. Just as the governing body is a "critical friend" of the school, so the local authority should be a "critical friend" to the governing body. Not only does the LA have the statutory duty to provide training and information for governors, but they also have the right to intervene in a school "in inverse proportion to success". In consequence, your LA should have a clearly understood monitoring framework based on schools' performance data.

When things start to go wrong with a school the LA has a number of options. LAs should have a monitoring system in place which includes collecting school performance data. Usually an early warning system indicates a school at risk, which becomes a "priority school", entitling it to a support package from the authority. If things fail to get better then a formal warning can be issued to the school requiring certain improvements. At this time the LA has the power to appoint additional governors to assist the governing body. If schools are designated as being in difficulty by Ofsted – either given a notice to improve* or judged in need of special measures* – then the LA also comes in with a support package, which can again include additional governors.

Getting and giving information

These circumstances should be extraordinary, and most governors will not face them. But in building a constructive relationship with the LA governors should think about what information and support they would like from the LA, and in turn the LA can request information from the governing body.

For example, you should consider asking the LA for comparative information about other schools in the authority in relation to any of its responsibilities. Comparative performance data can be helpful for target-setting. It can also be helpful in setting performance objectives for the headteacher (however, this is a sensitive issue and information may only be given in confidence). For community schools, in its legal capacity as employer, the LA should be able to offer information and assistance regarding pay policy and staffing levels, and as the admissions authority, should provide information and support on admissions. Financial management is one area where many schools rely heavily on LA professional support, and this should extend to the governing body, particularly in the budget-setting process. When you are setting the budget and deciding on which services to buy, the LA should be able to offer information and advice about the educational supply market. Some authorities offer a "brokerage" support service and will give information on service specification. The LA should also be able to help and advise schools wishing to cluster together to buy goods or services or to provide extended services. For schools involved in private finance initiatives, legal and financial advice for the governing body is essential and the LA is the best place to start, even if they then direct you to specialist support.

In any of these areas, the LA could also ask you for reports on the school's progress. With "best value" inspection of local authorities, and internal overview and scrutiny committee reviews, which require consultation with service users, you may also find yourselves providing information and evidence in support of continuous improvement in

→ pages 63-4

→ pages 58–9, 116

service provision. (Since the Local Government Act 2000 LAs have had overview and scrutiny committees which review issues of local concern, including, for example, how Every Child Matters provision is being offered.)

Any such dialogues with the LA will probably take place around the governing body meeting. Your governing body may be clerked by someone from your LA's clerking service, who may well know the personnel best able to give you the information and advice you want, but even if you have your own clerk, think about who you might like to invite from the LA to assist you, and when. In turn, the LA has the right to request (but cannot insist) that an officer or adviser attend the meeting if there are concerns which need to be brought to your attention. The LA also has the right to appoint an officer to take part in the selection procedure of a new headteacher or deputy of a community or voluntary controlled school; governors of foundation and voluntary aided schools can request such representation.

A significant area which demonstrates the importance of dialogue between the governing body and the LA is health and safety. The legal responsibility for health and safety in schools is shared between the LA and you. In order to fulfil its responsibility the LA should have a written policy and appoint an officer responsible for health and safety in schools. Schools should draw up their own policies, but these should adhere to the LA policy and are under an obligation to follow any instructions issued by the LA – but you should have the opportunity to discuss the LA's policy with them so that it is appropriate for your school.

In the interests of public accountability

Health and Safety

While day-to-day responsibility for the health and safety of pupils, staff and the educational environment rests with the headteacher – assisted often by a school co ordinator – they are accountable to the governing body. You must ensure that all reasonable steps are being taken to ensure no-one is put at risk and that all procedures, like that for reporting accidents, are in place and working. The LA has the right to request health and safety reports and assessment in order to fulfil their statutory duties, and you have the right to request information and support from the appropriate LA officers to enable you to carry out your responsibilities.

the relationship with the LA needs to be given due care and attention – in just the same way as the relationship between the governing body and the school.

Accountability to the state

The accountability for raising standards doesn't end with the local authority. The state, in the shape of the Office for Standards in Education, Children's Services and Skills (Ofsted), or Estyn in Wales, also rightly needs to know how things are going. Much has been written about the rights and wrongs of the Ofsted "regime", but the evidence is clear that a state inspection system, albeit with a lighter touch than it had originally, is a very necessary mechanism in ensuring that standards are maintained and improved.

While its role is essentially a form of professional accountability, the governing body has an important role to play in facilitating the inspection process. And remember that although the governing body is not part of the professional management of the school, it is also under scrutiny in the inspection process. Make sure that when the time comes you have made adequate preparation – which should just be good practice anyway. (Details of what Ofsted is looking at in inspections is available in the current edition of *Framework for the Inspection of Schools*, which Ofsted publishes itself, and which can be consulted on its website.)

Accountability to the public

→ pages 100–103

As outlined above, there are statutory formal requirements for the governing body to account to parents annually. More generally, though, an important component of delegated management is the requirement of schools to publish information about themselves and the achievement of their pupils. On the basis that parents expressing their preference of a school for their child need to have access to information in to make informed choices, schools are required to publish national test and examination results each year. These include data that compares the school with local and national results, in what have become known as the much publicised and discussed "league tables". (This is just in England. Wales does not have league tables any more.) These results are already supplied for English schools in the School Profile before schools download them for completion. It is also a statutory requirement for each school to produce a prospectus. Requirements of what has to be included change so the DCSF sets out regulatory guidance.

You should also be aware that the governing body's business is open to public scrutiny. Although your meetings are not open unless the governing body declares them so, minutes of meetings are public documents, together with any reports and information supplied. A copy of all relevant documents should be kept in the school for public record. Some governing bodies actually invite scrutiny by displaying their minutes on a public notice board, and this can be particularly helpful for parents. This means, of course, that any items which are to remain confidential should be noted in the minutes and recorded separately.

The use of the internet by local authorities and government departments, and the passing of the Freedom of Information Act, has widened access to public documents, and Ofsted reports, for example, are all published on its website. As the momentum for more open government gathers pace, you may find that more members of the public wish to see your documents too, so public access to them should be made easy.

For voluntary aided and foundation schools, accountability to the public also includes the foundation body. For church schools this is usually the local diocese, but the foundation can be a charitable trust, such as the Cadbury Trust for the Bourneville Schools in Birmingham, or the Kingshurst Trust set up to run schools modelled on the Kingshurst City Technology College model. In such cases the foundations are the majority stakeholder in the school, and a significant sponsor; they need to be satisfied that the school is meeting all its obligations to students.

Handling complaints and appeals

The governing body also has an important role to play as the final arbiter in complaints and appeals. This is a critical function which also forms part of public accountability.

It is a legal requirement for governing bodies to have a complaints policy which clearly sets out the procedures that should be followed if a parent or member of the public has a complaint. Schools are encouraged to have a complaints officer, who may be the headteacher, to investigate any formal complaint. Most complaints would be dealt with by the complaints officer in the school, but members of the governing body or the chair may be brought in as part of an appeals process.

→ pages 86–7 The governing body also has an appeals function with regard to staff grievances and staff dismissal proceedings. The power to dismiss staff resides with the headteacher. If the staff member appeals the governing body is statutorily obliged to form a panel to hear the appeal. Similarly, it has to form an appeals panel if a staff member appeals against a pay decision.

As the legal employer of staff in community and voluntary controlled schools, the LA should be able to give advice and support to governors dealing with staff grievance and dismissal and should have a staff grievance policy which your school could follow.

Governors also have a role to play in hearing appeals from pupils and parents against any decision made by the head-
→ page 86 teacher to exclude a child from the school. Here again the governing body has a statutory duty to form a Pupil Discipline Committee or exclusion panel to deal with such matters. It is important that the governing body carries out this function carefully and ensures that both pupil and parent are informed of the grounds for the decision and given a chance to put their case.

DCSF guidance sets out procedures to be followed in dismissing staff or examining exclusions, but advice should also be available from the LA, who will usually be called upon in such committee hearings. The LA should also be able to provide you with a copy of their own complaints' policy on which it is sensible to base your school's policy.

Individual governors are, of course, elected or appointed, which suggests that each individual governor might be accountable to their constituency or appointing body. However, individual governor responsibility and accountability have rightly been subsumed by the corporate nature of school governance. Since individual governors have no authority other than by virtue of their membership of the corporate body, it has been argued that any responsibility is exercised on behalf of the corporate body and therefore it is of that body only that accountability should be required.

And finally...

This begs the question of what the proper relationship is between individually appointed or elected governors and those who appoint or elect them. The law is clear that governors are not delegates but representatives of different stakeholder groups. The contribution of the "different voices" of the parent, the teacher and other governors to the deliberations on, for example, the staffing complement, the budget, the School Development Plan or target-setting, is the scaffolding for the stakeholder model of governance. Such public deliberation is the very rationale for the public governance of schools within a system of devolved management and governance.

So how do you, as an individual governor, ensure that your voice reflects those of your constituency or appointing body – and how do they know what contribution you are making on their behalf? The law offers no help here – nor do custom and practice. Indeed, conventional wisdom suggests that you are positively discouraged from seeking greater connection with a stakeholder group. All governors, once elected or appointed, are regarded equally with no distinctions (apart from staff being more restricted than other governors by the personal interest rules). Nevertheless, some parent governors have held surgeries, produced newsletters or sought a high profile at parents' evenings. Some teacher governors also formally keep colleagues informed. LAs are encouraged to try to ensure that the most appropriately qualified individuals are appointed and then supported in their role, which suggests a more visible relationship between LA appointees and the LA than has often been the case.

It seems that in an effort to deter any politicisation of the governing body, the message has been strongly communicated in recent years that all governors should somehow deny their constituencies or appointing bodies. But if governors are to have equal voices that are truly representative and do not assert only their own personal interests and concerns, then some form of accountability would seem to be appropriate. Such forms of accountability would require regular communication and consultation so that the view of the parent body, LA, church or other group could be more properly taken into account. In order to achieve this, you would need to be able to make contact in face-to-face meetings, newsletters or surveys. As we have seen, parent councils are compulsory in trust schools where the trust appoints the majority of the governing body, but they could benefit other schools too, providing a representative parent body that governors can consult.

But these means of contact are essentially political mechanisms, which invite more sustained political participation by the constituents or appointers than just a vote every four years. School governance does, indeed, involve making decisions about the future of the school that are inescapably political. For example, trust school status – will the governing body benefit from the extra powers, does the trust have an ethos that the school needs, should the link with the LA be lost? Smart targets and performance management – by whose standards: the government's, the LA's, the school's, the parents' or the pupils'?

Effective governance, particularly at a time when governors are making big decisions about the school, requires serious deliberations with all stakeholders, honestly and with confidence. Of course, this requires corporate trust and loyalty, but it also requires respect for different contributions that are confidently based on stakeholder views. Constructive and effective communication and consultation with stakeholder groups, either on an ongoing basis or in relation to particular issues, would be the best way of securing this. As you make your contribution to the discussions and debates about the nature of governance, this may be the greatest challenge for the future.

Conclusion

Over the years we have met many governors between us, often in a training context where we have been trying to help them to do a better job. There are many people with a lot of skills involved in governance, and nearly every governor brings a good deal of common sense to the task. But on almost every occasion people ask for greater clarity about what the task is. It seems particularly difficult to keep your eye on the ball of what is essential about governance when there is yet another initiative to contemplate or problem to solve. If we are to get beyond the urgent to the important, we must continue to watch the ball.

In this book we have tried to focus on three key concepts that are essential to the governing of a school. They are:

- public accountability

- strategic leadership

- governors as agents of change.

Many of the debates about the differences between governing and managing end up being territorial and sterile. We believe that schools that acknowledge a model of leadership that is jointly one of the head, or wider leadership team, and a committed governing body are likely to find a more fruitful way forward. We are convinced that for the most part governors do not need to manage but are part of the strategic leadership of the school, helping to set its direction and leading it into the future, which is likely to be one of constant change.

Strategic leadership is about looking forward, outwards and onwards – seeing the future, and inspiring others. The governing body has a huge motivational role to play in the school as part of the process towards change and improvement. We would urge every governing body to

• make their voice heard

• build bridges

• take calculated risks

• think outside the box

• to have an impact on the whole experience of the child

So we encourage you to be strategic ... be accountable ... be bold, and have fun while you do it.

Jane Martin and Ann Holt

Acknowledgements

This book has been the product of many lively discussions between ourselves and countless governors. We would like to acknowledge all those who share our passion for what we think is one of the most valuable pieces of community service that anyone can do. Most especially we want to thank Stephen Adamson, our editor, for his wise counsel and his extreme patience as we have put this book together. He is the one who believed that we had something important to say and has made it possible. We would also like to thank our partners, Stewart and Douglas, who put up with the unsocial hours and times away that it takes for us to indulge our passion for encouraging good governance on behalf of the young people in our schools.

Appendix

1. Mission

What is it currently? Use your vision, mission and overall aims statements to fill this in.

GOALS	SUCCESS INDICATORS

2. The learning perspective

3. The internal perspective

Takes account of the needs of all who learn and work in the school

Balanced scorecard pro-forma

	GOALS	SUCCESS INDICATORS

4. The external perspective

Who are our key interest groups? What do they expect?

5. The financial perspective

What is our budget? Are there other funds to tap into?

How do we do it? Our strategic objectives

1

2

3

4

5

6

Glossary

Advanced skills teacher: a teacher who is judged to teach to a particularly high standard. Advanced skills teachers receive extra pay and are expected to share their practice and methods with other teachers, both in their own school and in nearby schools. The category was introduced to spread good practice and to reward high-quality teachers who do not wish to go into management.

Annual Parents' Meeting: (Wales only) every year the governing body has to be prepared to hold a meeting that is open to all parents. Its main purpose is to receive and discuss the Annual Report. The governing body may write to parents saying that it thinks the meeting is not necessary, and unless 15 or more parents respond asking for it, it does not have to be held.

Annual Report to Parents: (Wales only) the governing body must produce a report once a year, which has to be sent to all parents at least two weeks before the Annual Parents' Meeting.

Benchmark: benchmarking is much used in assessing how well schools are performing. It consists of obtaining quantifiable information about the performance of other schools of a similar nature in terms of size, social mix, ethnic mix and funding. These can then be used as a yardstick for judging your own school's results.

Best value: all local authorities have to conduct reviews of their services to see whether they are providing value in terms of cost and quality. Best value is not just about securing goods or services at the cheapest price, but involves looking at the nature of what you are doing and deciding whether you should re-organise things so that your purchasing needs are different. Schools are not subject to formal review, but are expected to follow the principles behind best value. This means applying the four Cs to any purchasing decision: consult with those who are going to use the services, compare your school with what others are doing, assess competition by market testing, and challenge what you are doing to see if there is a better way.

Chair's action: the chair of a governing body can be asked to undertake tasks on behalf of the governing body, providing that these are ones that can legally be delegated. In emergencies, where the safety or welfare of a pupil, member of staff or the premises are threatened, a chair can take action without reference to the governing body. All actions undertaken by the chair, whether under delegation or in an emergency, should be reported to the next meeting of the governing body.

Committees: governing bodies may appoint what committees they wish, or none at all. The only obligatory committees or panels are those that hear appeals by teachers against dismissal or a pay decision (*staff appeals committee*) and examine permanent and lengthy fixed-term exclusions (*pupil discipline committee*). There also has to be a small panel of governors who conduct the headteacher's performance review. Committees differ from working groups and working parties in that the governing body delegates to them the power to make decisions on its behalf.

Curriculum: the curriculum covers all the things that pupils are taught at school. At the core is the National Curriculum, which prescribes the subjects that have to be taught, but a school will teach other subjects as well.

Every Child Matters: originally the title of a document published by the government in 2004, Every Child Matters is now the name given to one of the key agendas for education in England and Wales. It intends that every child should receive the education they need, should be healthy and secure, be equipped to face adult life with confidence and have a strong regard for community values. These aims are listed in "Five Outcomes" that are desired from education, and are embodied in law in the Children Act 2004. Every Child Matters

was framed in the wake of the Victoria Climbié inquiry because of a recognition that some children were failed by the system, largely because schools, social services and health services all acted independently of each other, without sharing information.

Excellence in Cities: scheme set up by the government to raise standards in schools in certain inner city areas where education achievements have traditionally been poor. Schools form networks across LAs, and benefit from extra funding to provide learning mentors, learning support units and support for gifted pupils.

Excellent Teachers: the Excellent Teacher post was created in 2005 to reward teachers who have reached the top of the Upper Pay Spine but whose teaching standards continue to improve and who wish to take on further responsibility without taking on a management role. An Excellent Teacher is not only expected to provide a very good quality of teaching but is required to share their skills and knowledge with their colleagues.

Fast-Track teachers: each year a number of trainee teachers, who are considered to have exceptional promise, are employed from universities and training colleges on a special scheme which is expected to see them gain rapid promotion. They receive intensive on-the-job training, and should change school every two years or so in order to broaden their experience of teaching. They also receive more pay than other newly qualified teachers; this is funded by central government.

Guide to the Law: full title *A Guide to the Law for School Governors*. Published by the DCSF this is distributed free to all school governors. It explains the legal responsibilities of governors, organised into 22 subjects. A single guide is published for all maintained schools, with differences flagged between community, community special, foundation, foundation special, voluntary aided and voluntary controlled schools. The most up-to-date edition is on the GovernorNet website.

Headteacher's report: the headteacher should give a written report to the governing body at least once a term. The report should cover: progress on the School Development Plan, staffing issues, resources, finance, health and safety, performance indicators such as examination and SATs results, school visits and visitors to the school. It provides an important opportunity for governors to monitor the school's progress and ask questions.

Home-school agreement: all schools have to a have a written agreement that each parent is asked to sign. The agreement is meant to describe what parents and school expect of each other. It should include the school's ethos, the standard of education, the importance of regular and punctual attendance by pupils, required behaviour and disciplinary measures, homework, and the information parents and school give each other. The agreement should be revised from time to time, in consultation with the parents.

Key Stage: with the introduction of the National Curriculum school education was phased into a number of Key Stages. Pupils in years 1 and 2 (ages five to seven) are Key Stage 1, pupils in years 3 to 6 are Key Stage 2 (ages seven to eleven), pupils in years 7 to 9 are Key Stage 3 (ages eleven to fourteen) and those in years 10 and 11 are Key Stage 4 (ages fourteen to sixteen). All pupils in England are tested at the end of each Key Stage, while at the end of Key Stage 4 pupils are expected to take GCSEs.

Local management of schools: term introduced by the 1986 Education Act to describe the devolution of responsibility from LAs to individual schools. Under local management governing bodies became responsible for their own budgets.

Maintained schools: the official term for what are commonly known as 'state schools'. All maintained schools are funded in large part by their local education authority.

Mission statement: a mission statement gives an organisation a sense of purpose and direction. It should consist of three elements: the vision (where you want to go), the route (how you propose to get there) and the values and principles underlying your vision.

National Curriculum: the National Curriculum specifies various subjects that have to be taught in schools. These fall into core and non-core subjects. The core subjects are English, maths and science (plus Welsh in Wales), and the non-core are design and technology, information and communications technology, history, geography, modern foreign languages (Key

Stage 3), art and design, music, physical education and citizenship (Key Stages 3 and 4). History, geography, art and design and music are not compulsory at Key Stage 4. Religious education must also be provided.

Notice to improve: in their report the Ofsted inspectors may determine that a school is inadequate in various respects. It will describe the weaknesses, which the headteacher and governors are expected to to address. They should aim to redress the weaknesses within one year. The school will meet termly with the LA to discuss progress, and will be visited again by inspectors after one year. The inspectors will either declare that the school has successfully removed the weaknesses or will put it on special measures.

Ofsted: to April 2007 the Office for Standards in Education; after that the Office for Standards in Education, Children's Services and Skills. A department of government responsible for inspecting schools, local authority Children's Services departments and certain colleges.

Parent governor representative: to make local authorities more accountable to parents, in 2000 the government specified that each local council education committee should have between two and five representatives of local parents, in addition to the elected councillors. With the restructuring of local councils these representatives now sit on the committee that scrutinises education. The representatives are elected from among serving parent governors throughout the authority's schools.

Performance management: system of appraisal and target-setting for staff. Governors are responsible for conducting the performance review of the headteacher. The review of the rest of the staff is the responsibility of the headteacher, who may well delegate to individual line managers. The governing body has to draw up a policy for the performance management of all staff.

Regulations: many of the rules determining governors' responsibilities and how governing bodies must discharge them are not contained in Acts of Parliament, but in separate regulations. These are drawn up by the DCSF and are submitted to Parliament for approval. They then have the force of law. *See also* **School Governance (Constitution) Regulations** *and* **Terms of Reference regulations.**

School advisers: LAs employ a number of experts whose job is to help schools conduct their business. They will normally be specialists in a curriculum area or a level of schooling, such as nursery or secondary. A lot of their work is being taken over by School Improvement Partners (SIPs), and, indeed, in primary schools a lot of SIPs are local authority advisers. Governors are also likely to work with financial advisers.

School Development Plan: key document in defining a school's priorities. It should describe what governors and teachers want the school to achieve over a number of years – usually three – and detail how and when it will fulfil these aims. The SDP should contain a good level of detail, especially for the immediate year, and should be revised annually.

School Governance (Constitution) Regulations, The : these regulations determine the composition of governing bodies and how governing bodies should conduct their business. There are different regulations for England and Wales.

School Improvement Partners (SIPs): in response to complaints from headteachers that they were having to have meetings with too many advisers from local authorities and other official bodies, the government announced in 2004 that it would help reduce these by creating the post of School Improvement Partner for each school. The headteacher would be able to discuss issues with this person, particularly about the school's standards, that had previously involved conversations with many separate people. In secondary schools most SIPs are serving or recent headteachers, while in primary schools the majority are taken from amongst the advisers they replace. SIPs also advise governing bodies on headteachers' performance reviews.

School Improvement Plan: alternative name for the School Development Plan.

School Profile: in 2006 the School Profile replaced the governors' annual report for parents in England. Governors have to provide, or supervise the provision of, information on matters such as the character of the school, the curriculum it offers, and how it works with parents and the community. Key statistical information on the academic results is supplied by the DCSF. The form is an on-line document, and when complete governors should inform parents and tell them where they can access it.

School Standards Grant: a lump sum paid each year directly by government to schools, without strings attached

Self Evaluation Form (SEF): form schools are expected to complete and/or revise at least annually in which they evaluate their own performance. The form is the basis of an inspection by Ofsted, but should be completed even when an inspection is not thought imminent.

Special measures: a school that is deemed by Ofsted to be failing to deliver an adequate standard of education will be placed on special measures. The headteacher and governors together with the LA must produce an action plan showing how it intends to improve the areas identified in the report as being poor. The school receives regular visits from Ofsted inspectors to monitor progress. They may decide at any time that the school has improved sufficiently to be taken off special measures, but if after one year progress has not been sufficient the school may be closed.

Stakeholder: any person or group who has a direct interest in the performance of an organisation.

Standard Assessment Tests: SATs is the term commonly used for tests taken by pupils at the end of Key Stages 1, 2 and 3. The term is unofficial though extremely widespread; it does not appear in DCSF publications, where the tests are referred to as "National Curriculum assessment tests".

Standards Fund: Standards Fund money is paid directly to schools, and hence is unaffected by LA budget calculations. The fund consists of a number of grants, covering specific topics considered to contribute directly to the raising of standards, such as staff training, information and training for governors, and developing social inclusion. Schools have to apply for each grant that they want.

SWOT analysis: a tool often used by management consultants and others to get managers to think strategically about their company or organisation. The term is an acronym for four aspects of the organisation you consider: its strengths, its weaknesses, the opportunities it faces and the threats it confronts.

Teachers' pay scale: teachers' salaries are on one of two "spines", their position on each being determined by their experience and their responsibilities. The basic spine covers qualified teachers in their first few years of employment, and teachers can expect to move up one spine point each year. Those who have reached the top of the scale, normally after five years, can then apply to be assessed to see whether they should cross the "threshold" and move onto the upper pay scale, which has two spine points. After that they can apply for Excellent Teacher positions. Teachers in the leadership group – the senior managers – are on a different pay scale, as are headteachers.

Teaching and Learning Responsibilities (TLRs): management posts in schools that include line management responsibilities but focus on teaching and learning. There are two grades.

Terms of reference of committees: any non-statutory committee set up by the governing body to which it delegates decision-making powers must have its constitution, remit and method of appointing its chair determined by the governing body. The governing body also decides whether it can include non-governors, and if so whether they can vote. These terms of reference must be examined and confirmed or revised each year.

Terms of Reference regulations: called in full The Education (School Government) (Terms of Reference) (England) Regulations 2000, these regulations defined the respective roles of the head and the governing body. They have since been superseded by legislation, but their principles, in updated form, remain in the DCSF's Governing Body Decision Planner, on the GovernorNet website.

Threshold: see **Teachers' pay scale**

Timed agenda: an agenda which includes an indication of the amount of time that should be spent on each item.

Working parties/groups: working parties differ from committees in that they do not have any decision-making powers. As they merely submit reports or make recommendations to the governing body, they can contain any number of non-governors.

Selected bibliography

Code of Practice – LEA School Relations, DfEE, 1999 (ISBN 1 841850 08 X)

Education (School Government) (Terms of Reference) (England) Regulations 2000, The, no. 2122

Governing Body Decision Planner, www.governornet.co.uk

Guide to the Law for School Governors, A, DCSF, regularly updated - also available on line on www.governornet.co.uk

Lessons in Teamwork, Audit Commission/Ofsted, HMSO, 1995

Manual for Governing Bodies and their Clerks, A, ISCG, 2003

NGA Papers (there are various, such as *Governors: who they are and what they do, Effective Governors Meetings* and *Staff Selection*), National Governors' Association

Performance Management Framework, The, DfEE, 2000, ref: DfEE 0051/2000

Performance Management Guidance for Governors, DfEE, 2000

School Governors' Yearbook, The Adamson Publishing, annual

Addresses

The following organisations are referred to in the text or bibliography of this book.

Adamson Publishing: 8 The Moorings, Norwich NR3 3AX; tel 01603 623336, fax 01603 624767, e-mail: info@adamsonbooks.com, website: www.adamsonbooks.com

Department for Children, Schools and Families (DCSF): Sanctuary Buildings, Great Smith Street, London SW1P 3BT; tel 0870 0012345, e-mail: dcsf.gsi.gov.uk, website: www.dcsf.gov.uk

DCSF Publications Centre: PO Box 2093, London E3 3SQ; tel 0845 602 2260, fax 0845 603 3360, website: www.dcsf.gov.uk

Estyn (Office of the Chief Inspector of Schools, Wales): Anchor Court, Keen Road, Cardiff, CF24 5JW; tel 029 2044 6446, fax 029 2044 6448, website: www.estyn.gov.uk

Governors Wales: Empire House, 1st floor, Mount Stuart Square, Cardiff Bay, Cardiff, CF10 5FN; tel 029 2048 7858, fax 029 2048 7843, e-mail: governorswales@btconnect

Information for School and College Governors (ISCG): Avondale Park School, Sirdar Road, London W11 4EE; tel 020 7229 0200, fax 020 7229 0651, e-mail: iscg-contact@compuserve.com

National Assembly for Wales: Cardiff Bay, Cardiff, CF99 1NA; tel 029 20 898200, fax: 029 20 898229, website: www.wales.gov.uk

National Governors' Association (NGA): SBQ1, 29 Smallbrook Queensway, Birmingham B5 4 HG; tel 0121 643 5787, fax 0121 633 7141, e-mail: governorhq@nga.org.uk, website: www.nga.org.uk

Office for Standards in Education, Children's Services and Skills (OFSTED): Alexandra House, 33 Kingsway, London WC2B 6SE; tel 020 7421 6800, fax 020 7421 6707, e-mail: ofsted.gtnet.gov.uk, website: www.ofsted.gov.uk

Stationery Office, The: PO Box 29, Norwich NR3 1GN; tel 020 7873 0011, fax 0870 600 5533, e-mail: book-enquiries@theso.co.uk, website: www.clickso.com

Index

For terms with several references the main one is given in bold type.

The authors

Ann Holt has wide experience of both being a governor and training governors. She was the first director of Action for Governors' Information and Training and has been a special adviser to the DfES, working particularly on Performance Management. In 2004 she was awarded an OBE for services to education, having worked in the sector for over thirty years. She is much in demand as a speaker at conferences nationally and internationally. Her current role is that of executive director of the Bible Society (England and Wales).

Dr Jane Martin was the first director of the Centre for Public Scrutiny (CfPS) from 2003 until October 2006 when she took up the post of Senior Research Fellow in Public Leadership at the Institute of Governance and Public Management in Warwick Business School. A former local authority officer responsible for school governance, she has researched and written widely on education and school governance issues. She has had many years experience as a school governor in both primary and secondary schools, and has acted as an adviser to a number of government departments and national bodies.